AN EFFECTIVE GUIDE ON HOW TO ANALYZE AND PERSUADE PEOPLE SPEED READING THEIR BODY LANGUAGE AND BEHAVIOUR

(Human Psychology, Manipulation Tecniques, Mind Control, Dark Psychology)

by

Jacob K. Darren

Disclaimer

The information contained in this eBook is offered for informational purposes solely, and it is geared towards providing exact and reliable information in regards to the topic and issue covered. The author and the publisher does not warrant that the information contained in this e-book is fully complete and shall not be responsible for any errors or omissions.

The author and publisher shall have neither liability nor responsibility to any person or entity concerning any reparation, damages, or monetary loss caused or alleged to be caused directly or indirectly by this e-book. Therefore, this eBook should be used as a guide - not as the ultimate source.

The publication is sold with the idea that the publisher is not required to render accounting, officially permitted, or otherwise, qualified services. If advice is necessary, legal or professional, a practiced individual in the profession should be ordered.

In no way is it legal to reproduce, duplicate, or transmit any part of this document in either electronic means or printed format. Recording of

© Jacob K. Darren

Table of Content

© Jacob K. Darren

Analyze and Persuade People

Introduction

Thank you for downloading the "**An Effective Guide on How to Analyze and Persuade People Speed Reading their Body Language and Behaviour** ". This book has been strategically written and divided into two significant definite aspects that help with analyzing other people and how to persuade them to do what you want.

Do you want to read peoples mind? Do you want to know how to understand people instantly? Many scientists and experts say that it is impossible to read the mind of people and follow them by just looking at them. They are right, and you will never know that person unless you talked to him a lot, go with him often and hung out with him.

In marketing and sales, it is essential that you can read people instantly because you are not going to meet just one person per day. You will never go anywhere by that.

There is one powerful tool that will help you read people instantly and instantly you can get what you want. The tool is not a thing, it is in you, and you just need to develop it. It is the power and art of persuasion that is hidden in you.

Analyze and Persuade People

Every one of us has its hidden persuasion. You just need to exercise and train yourselves on how to use them primarily reading people.

Reading people instantly is not that easy, but with the power of persuasion, you will learn how to read people immediately. You will learn that persuasive technique in here.

The power of persuasion can help you pull out something from the affluent, and that's how you are going to read and understand them.

There are different ways on how you can read people but only this art of persuasion that you can read them instantly. Like for example, you can read people through their body language. You will know if that person is interested in you by his body language. Another example that you can read people but only these powers of persuasion you can pull them out instantly are the facial expressions and eye movement. Just the facial expression, you can read a lot from that.

Your persuasion technique will help you determine what's with that expression, did they understand you, and do they believe in you or trust you? Your persuasion and how you persuade people will answer that question instantly.

Analyzing People

Emotional Intelligence

People think no one knows them like the way they do. People maintain that they are more familiar with their houses than anybody else is.

They assert that they have far more knowledge about their neighbourhood when compared with others. People just like to profess that they understand their lives inside out. On the other hand, about emotions and personalities, the truth is quite contrary to what is stated.

We are inclined to turn a blind eye about our failings. We would like to believe that we are aware of our emotions and personalities well, but the fact is that a majority of people overlook their shortcomings.

For instance, let us take emotional intelligence. When a person gets to know about the significance of EI, without much ado, he starts to dwell on people whom he feels are bereft of emotional intelligence. Not many people take the trouble to look at themselves to find out if they are devoid of EI.

It is for this reason that a person requires undergoing intelligence tests. Now, a person should understand just to what extent the matter of emotional intelligence tends to shape his life.

The best possible way to make someone realize his limitations is to cause them to become conscious of it. Now, if somebody came near you just now and stated that you were without EI, is it possible for you to accept it as real?

A person has to be presented evidence regarding his failings before he is convinced.

The advantage of tests on emotional intelligence lies in the fact that these tests give you an opportunity to confirm directly how right you were about the observation of yourself.

By going through a test on emotional intelligence, you may expose yourself to the likelihood that you do not just know yourself the way you believe you do.

This alteration in assessment makes it easier for you to modify your way of thinking with the intention that you become more aware of the need to change for the better.

Analyze and Persuade People

A further benefit of undertaking a test on emotional intelligence is that it makes it possible for a person to identify precisely that particular portion of emotional intelligence that he is found wanting. Using a test of emotional knowledge, it is possible for a person to gather as to which section of emotional intelligence needs his attention.

Emotional intelligence tests, besides, make it easy for someone to appreciate the prospect of possessing emotional intelligence. By way of these EI tests, a person discovers how to avail himself of emotional intelligence, each day of his life. Due to this, a person can lead a far more contented and successful life.

Moreover, emotional intelligence tests too can enlighten a person just to what extent he can connect with other people.

Now, the social interface can prove to be enormously significant in one's life. This is dead right. You could be either an employee or a student, but you require others to lend a hand as you travel down life's way.

Tests on emotional intelligence can assist you to improve your aptitude to sense the way other people feel. This attitude enables you to identify with those around you. Insight is the basis of knowledge. When you are capable of securing some awareness about a person's emotions, then you should not have any difficulty in counting him as part of your inner circle.

Tests on emotional intelligence are lovely since they permit a person to observe the facts. It is common knowledge that the top barrier to truth is found in one's self. A test on emotional intelligence can negotiate a person's resistance and permit that person to assess himself without prejudice.

NLP Eye Accessing Cues

NLP eye accessing cues give the adage "eyes are the windows to the soul" a whole new meaning. This means that the direction in which our eyes move reveals whether we're remembering something or imagining something new.

By learning about these different cues, you can drastically improve your current persuasion skills. You should try and read this to find out how NLP eye accessing cues can help you in understanding people's minds and persuading people to do what you want.

To start with, you must first learn which eye cues correspond to the different senses.

If a person is trying to remember or recall an image, their eyes will probably move up to their left. If a person is trying to imagine or "visually construct" a new image, their eyes will step up to their right.

If a person is trying to remember a sound, their eyes will most likely turn to their immediate left. If a person is trying to imagine how a group of musical notes, for example, would sound like, their eyes will move to their immediate right.

Other parts of our senses, as well as your emotions, also have different NLP eye accessing cues. If a person is dealing with smell, tastes, touch and emotions, their eyes will probably move to their downward right. And if a person is talking to himself or herself mentally (or otherwise), the eyes will most likely move downward left.

Application Of NLP Eye Accessing Cues

Equipping yourself with this information helps you spot whether a person is lying through their teeth or entertaining a new idea. So let's say you ask someone, "Where were you when the child fell?" If they look up to the right, they might be making up a story to cover the real incident. If they look up to the left, they might be recalling what happened (in reality).

This method may help you determine if you want to accept their explanation or not, while also taking into account other factors.

You can also take advantage of this information to appear more honest or trustworthy. For example, if you want your story to seem more believable, make sure to follow the right NLP eye accessing cues to come across as genuine.

Knowing these cues by heart can also come quite handy in selling. If your target, for example, finds himself or herself having an internal dialogue about buying a brand new car, then you'll know that one way to persuade them is to present to them the pros and cons of making the bold purchase yourself (focusing more on the advantages, of course) and cutting off the customer's opportunity to convince himself or herself otherwise.

Analyze & Persuade People With Different Personalities

Proactive

If you want to know how to influence others, becoming familiar with personality types is a great skill to have. It will enable you to read other people like a book. You will understand what motivates them, what is going on inside their heads and how to push their buttons.

It is almost as if somebody hands you a manual and says: "Here if you want me to do something, this is how you will get me to do it."

There are many personality types, and one of them is proactive. Also, remember that the dynamic pattern is something that exists on a scale, of which the opposite is reactive.

A person is almost never only proactive, or just reactive, but somewhere on a scale between proactive and reactive.

Some people are more extreme to one side, some people are pretty balanced, and all of us can have different levels or pro- or reactivity depending on the situation and the context. So it is essential that you keep that in mind.

What Is A Proactive Person?

A proactive person is somebody who gets things started, and gets them done. Somebody who initiates action. Somebody who decides to do things and then does them. It is very different from people who think about and analyse things and wait for others to tell them what to do.

You can often recognise highly proactive people by their body language already. They tend to move a lot or tap with their pencil when they sit in a meeting or talk on the phone. They also often speak rather fast.

They speak in short sentences that have a clear sentence structure. They hardly ever use convoluted sentences.

They get to the point. And when they speak with somebody, they can be (and in fact often are) straightforward people, even to the point of stepping on other people's toes and upsetting them. Reactive people often think of them as "inconsiderate".

© Jacob K. Darren   [15]

How To Identify The Four Personality Types

There are four personality types or social styles Analytics, Drivers, Expressives and Amiables and all four have their unique approach to business, their language and thought processes etc. As a consequence, the very best sales professionals have become adept at recognising which personality they are dealing with and adapt their approach and communication style accordingly.

In every boardroom, you will always find three of the four personality types, occasionally, all four:

❖ **The Driver**

Let's begin by looking at the characteristics of the Driver. Drivers are action and goal oriented, need to see results and have a quick reaction time. They are decisive, independent, disciplined, practical and efficient. They typically use facts and data, speak and act quickly, lean forward, point and make direct eye contact. Their body posture is often rigid, and they have controlled facial expressions.

They rarely want to waste time on personal talk or preliminaries and can be perceived by other styles as dominating or harsh and severe in pursuit of a goal. They are comfortable in positions of power and control, and they have professional offices with certificates and commendations on the wall. In times of stress, drivers may become autocratic.

❖ **The Analytical**

Analytics is concerned with being organised, having all the facts and being careful before taking action. Their need is to be accurate, to be right. Precise, orderly, methodical and conform to standard operating procedures, organisational rules and historical ways of doing things. They typically have slow reaction time and work more slowly and carefully than Drivers. They are perceived as severe, industrious, persistent, and exacting.

Usually, they are task oriented, use facts and data, and tend to speak slowly. Lean back and use their hands frequently. They do not make direct eye contact and control their facial expressions. Others may see them as stuffy, indecisive, critical, picky and moralistic. They are comfortable in positions in which they can check facts and figures and be sure they are right. They have neat, well-organised offices and in times of stress, Analyticals tend to avoid conflict.

❖ **The Expressive**

Expressives enjoy involvement, excitement, and interpersonal action. They are sociable, stimulating, and enthusiastic and are good at involving and motivating others. They are also ideas oriented. Have little concern for routine, are future-oriented, and usually, they have a quick reaction time.

They need to be accepted by others, tend to be spontaneous, outgoing, energetic, and friendly and focused on people rather than on tasks. Typically, they use opinions and stories rather than facts and data. They speak and act quickly; vary vocal inflexion, lean forward, point and make direct eye contact.

They use their hands when talking; have a relaxed body posture and an animated expression. Their feelings often show in their faces, and they are perceived by others as excitable, impulsive, undisciplined, dramatic, manipulative, ambitious, overly reactive and egotistical. They usually have disorganised offices and may have leisure equipment like golf clubs or tennis racquets. Under stressful conditions, Expressives tend to resort to personal attack.

❖ **The Amiable**

Amiables need co-operation, personal security and acceptance. They are uncomfortable with and will avoid conflict at all costs. They value personal relationships, helping others and being liked. Some Amiables will sacrifice their desires to win approval from others.

They prefer to work with other people in a team effort, rather than individually and they have unhurried reaction time and little concern with effecting change. Typically, they are friendly, supportive, respectful, willing, dependable and agreeable. They are also people-oriented.

They use opinions rather than facts and data, speak slowly and softly, use more vocal inflexion than Drivers or Analytics. They lean back while talking and do not make direct eye contact; they also have a casual posture and an animated expression. They are perceived by other styles as conforming, unsure, pliable, dependent and awkward. They have homely offices family photographs, plants etc. An Amiable's reaction to stress is to comply with others.

Strengths And Weaknesses Of Personality Types

There are four basic personality types. While everyone has a bit of each of them, there is one that dominates. The four types, which is referred to as colours, are:

- ❖ Yellow - (phlegmatic, nurturer)
- ❖ Blue - (sanguine, fun-seeker)
- ❖ Green - (melancholy, analytical)
- ❖ Red - (choleric, money-driven)

Each type has strengths and weaknesses which hold right most of the time. You can maximise your success by using your strengths, especially in a team environment, and by improving in your weak areas.

The strengths of a Yellow are that they are dependable, patient team players who always want to help others. One weakness is that they tend to be overly sensitive and take comments (and rejection) too personally. They tend to be followers rather than leaders, and not goal-oriented.

Every leader must be a good follower first, but to be truly successful you must eventually step into leadership and set some goals. Yellows often get sidetracked from working on their business because they feel it is more important to spend time with their family, church or charitable causes.

While those things are essential, if you are building a home-based business you need to spend at least 10 hours a week on it to become successful. If it takes you 2 months to read a book that could change your life and your business, ask yourself why you keep putting it off. You deserve to achieve your dreams and should not sacrifice them to help others. Instead, help others in the process of obtaining your goals.

The strengths of a Blue are that they are great promoters, creative, and enthusiastic. One weakness is that sometimes their enthusiasm is too "over-the-top" and they may even exaggerate, which puts people off. They also tend to talk too much and not listen to others. While they are good at sponsoring people into a business, they often lack the organisation and follow-up to help the other person succeed.

The strengths of a Green are that they are organised, accurate, and persistent and they follow through.

Their main weakness is "analysis to paralysis." They want everything to be perfect, so they attempt to gather every possible piece of information before moving forward. They can be too slow at making decisions and let opportunities pass them by.

They are too dependent on proving things will work before getting started, instead of learning to take some things on faith.

They are sometimes also frugal, again wanting to determine in advance that their money will be well-spent instead of trying something and accepting some risk.

They take most things too seriously and can become lonely and depressed. Greens also tend to believe they are always right and are reluctant to admit when they are wrong, so they often hurt other people's feelings.

The strengths of a Red are that they are focused and goal-oriented. Their weaknesses are that they have a big ego, are short-tempered and impatient, and are not coachable.

It's "my way or the highway" with a red, and they don't care how many bodies they leave on the side of the road.

They just say "NEXT" and move on. They order people around instead of understanding the concept of "attracting more flies with honey." It is very intimidating.

You should try and make an honest assessment of yourself and continue to work on self-development, as it will help you succeed in any business.

If you are in a position to coach or supervise others this information is also invaluable! Recognizing other people's personality type can be learned relatively quickly with practice and will help you communicate more effectively with everyone you meet.

How To Communicate With Them

People express themselves in different ways because they have different characters. Some like to express themselves with a lot of joy whereas as others like to drive others to do something while others again like to use their analytical minds to analyse something.

From this short intro, it is clear that there are at least three types of people who use different ways to express themselves: expressers, drivers, and analysers.

❖ Expressers

These people are always in the joyful mood and like to ask about others. They like to know what others are doing and not what the outcome will be. They do not like complicated explanations to avoid losing the happy moments they have. They are genuinely social beings because they enjoy social life, mingling, interacting, and joking with everyone they meet.

They hate dry facts which only cause stress and will reduce their happiness. They are more inclined to do 'fun' things. They are straightforward and to the point. They do not like poems and old songs full of flowery words. They like things to be brief and clear.

When communicating with expressers try to follow their happy rhythm, show the same joy as they do, clap your hands if necessary avoid competing with them, give enthusiastic responses.

Acknowledge their professional achievements, react fast to their messages, and give them challenges which they will surely like. Always try to be happy when communication with them. They are simple people who dislike complicated things. By following their style, a harmonious relationship can be formed with them.

❖ **Drivers**

These kinds of people have a high drive to stimulate others to do things as they want them to be. It is essential to stay in control otherwise you might be doing only what they want. The best way to communicate with them is by letting them lead the beginning and end of the conversation. Let them explain in which direction they want to drive the conversation and let them decide what is best. Praise them gently and expose your message in between your praises. Show accommodating body language through shaking their hands and repeated nodding.

These people have bigger egos than the average person, and they feel that they are born to lead and drive others. For this reason, they are highly self-confident, and it is important to avoid hurting their egos. If this happens, you will not be able to repair this damage. Always follow them and smartly give your messages.

❖ **Analysers**

These people have a healthy analytic mind and use the left hemisphere of their brain in a very efficient way. They are logical and rational thinkers when analysing a problem.

They hate irrationality and unproven methods. When communicating with them, it is necessary to have the right data and facts to provide correct and valid information.

Talk about processes and not results and give them the freedom to make decisions. Do not blame them because they do not see themselves as making any mistakes. They are weak communicators because they are stiff and hate being criticised.

Facts and data will be everything for them and be using them will make communicating with them a natural thing.

Avoid using too many words when talking to them because they consider you to be wasting their valuable time. The best way to communicate with them is to relax, provide a lot of facts and data and let them decide what is best based on those facts.

Persuading Others After Analyzing Them

Most of the people don't know the importance of persuasion. They don't know that it is a very important skill in life. This is the only skill that can boost your sales and business, can make a happy family, can build a very strong relationship and can influence others and take them to your way of thinking. Having this kind of skill, you'll never know how easy life is.

Having this great persuasion skill in you is indeed an excellent advantage for you. Why? Well, you can easily court the woman you liked, and you can even earn more in your sales and marketing. But, somehow it is used in politics to win the peoples trust and even in courts. You can see now how useful this skill in life.

Now, let us focus on how we can persuade more people to boost up your business and your sales. In the world of business, persuasion is very helpful, especially in winning negotiations and taking your clients to take immediate actions.

Here are some ways that can help you persuade others.

Have you heard that saying 'do not do unto others what you do not want others to do unto you'? In business, this is 'do unto others what you want them to do unto you.'

The first persuasive ways to persuade people is to do good first to others so that they will also in return do good to you. This means that you give first to your clients or customers. It is very common that if we get a favor from others, it creates a need to return that favor. And we can use attitude in our advantage to persuade others.

Now, after you give, you can create a need, and you can easily follow persuading them. This need means a need for having your product. For example, 'Do you have trouble cleaning your house or does it take time to clean your whole house? Well, you can use this machine or product, and you can easily clean your house in just 1 hour'. Just like this, you are creating a need for your client to take action because they need your product to solve their problem in cleaning their house.

Analyze and Persuade People

Of course, without confidence, you can never do this job. With your power of persuasion, you must build up your confidence in the way you talk to your clients or customers. This confidence means that when you persuade others, you need to talk straight. You need to be consistent also for them to trust you.

Great persuaders are those having a very effective communication skill.

Before people can trust you, they want to see you as an example. You cannot bring others to do what you want if you have a bad attitude.

The choice of words in your persuasion is also very important. There are lots of words, powerful words that can easily persuade others.

Power Of Persuasion

The secret of the universe is the power of persuasion. Persuasion is the one key to getting what you want, becoming rich, and having success in anything. Without persuasion, nothing gets done. It is about persuading yourself and others. Persuasion is about moving consciousness, and when you can move consciousness, you can move anything in the universe. All persuasion is persuading to take action, whether mental or physical action. All wealthy and successful people are masters of persuasion.

You may have had certain ideas against using persuasion because you think it is manipulation. But those are limiting beliefs that you have which are stopping you from success. The use of persuasion for wrongful purposes is manipulation, but the natural use of persuasion is for direction. People want to be directed in a way that makes them eager and comfortable with taking action to benefit themselves. We all naturally want to be led into doing what's good for us by someone who can show us the way.

Analyze and Persuade People

Realize that perception creates reality. Persuasion is about changing the perception of people in order to change their reality. It is about helping others to see things in a different way that they didn't see before. In order to use persuasion, you first have to persuade yourself about the use of persuasion. You have to change your perception of persuasion. When you can shift your perception and beliefs about reality to those who're wealthy and successful, you can use the power of persuasion the way they use it.

The most powerful and influential people in the world are the persuaders. They have the power to shift people's perception, beliefs, and ideas about things. If you want to change the world, you have to change the consciousness of people. The most powerful kind of persuasion is persuasion that moves people in the direction that they already want to go. It is persuasion to show them the means of getting that which they desire. You can persuade people to do anything if they think it will satisfy them.

In all persuasion, the purpose is to persuade people that they have a certain desire, how they can satisfy that desire, and that it is worth what they give in exchange for that which will satisfy their desire. There are many places that teach persuasion in different ways, but the fundamental principles all come down to the few that represent them all. It is about getting attention and sparking interest and curiosity. Then it is about arousing desire and persuading them to take a certain action to fulfill that desire.

The key thing that all persuasion deals with is to convince others about the value of something. Something only has value according to the value that you give it. Who is to say that a particular product is worth a certain amount of money? The truth is that everything in the universe is free. All the things in life obtain their value from the perception of people. The perception of value can differ from one person to another. You can create any value in anything simply by how you cause others to perceive it.

Nothing in the universe is of any use to any being except by the consciousness that the being has towards it. All drugs medicines would not work to heal if a person believes that they would not improve, and their consciousness is not in harmony for healing but for the disease. For a person who has the consciousness and belief for healing, even a placebo would procure the effect of healing. No one can obtain satisfaction from anything unless they have the consciousness to obtain satisfaction from that thing.

It is persuasion that makes the world go round. If people are not persuaded to do anything, there would be no movement of energy. There would be no buying or selling. When resources are not being moved around, things cannot be placed into the hands of those who can put them to better use. The economy comes to a standstill when money is not flowing. When people keep what they have instead of giving it to obtain something more, it will only lead to stagnation, entropy, and degrading of the universe.

That is why the marketers and sales promoters are really doing society an excellent service. By persuading people to see value in something and to give something else, whether it is time, money, or resources in order to obtain it, they are promoting the exchange of energy. When energy is exchanged, that is when there can be new combinations and advanced forms of energy created for the rest of the world to benefit from. The exchange of energy is what supports the evolution of humanity and the advancement of life.

Analyze and Persuade People

Persuasion is the power that can move people to buy trash or treasure. If there are people who use very persuasive and compelling messages to influence people to buy trash, doesn't that give you all the reason to use the same kind of powerful persuasion to influence people to purchase treasure instead? You can sell them the moon, the stars and the galaxy when it comes to promoting what you have to offer, because the value is created by perception, and you're doing them a favor by leading them to yours instead.

Market forces are influenced by supply and demand. Even supply and demand is based on perception. You never have to worry about supply and demand when you can create demand through persuasion and persuade others to perceive you as their best supply. You can create your own market with the power of persuasion, and that is why it is called marketing. The ability to influence is the power to create wealth. When you can move consciousness, the world is your oyster, and it is yours for the taking.

The way to great wealth is to create as much value as possible for others. Since value is created by perception, you can create value by creating the perception of value. The greater the perception of the value you are able to create and the more people you are able to influence, the more you can create an exchange of energy where money flows to you in exchange for what you offer. You can have everything you want if you help others get what they want, which is by what you persuade them to want and get.

Persuasion Techniques

The power of persuasion can open doors for you and make the path to success much smoother. After reading this book, you will have an array of persuasive techniques at your disposal.

The most persuasive techniques have their roots in NLP (neuro-linguistic programming). These persuasion techniques are based on empathy - in order to persuade someone - you must understand them.

Empathy-Based Persuasive Techniques

The first and most important thing you must understand about the person you are trying to influence is what their mind best responds to - feel, visual, or auditory stimulation. Knowing this will allow you to be more persuasive by plugging into and feeding this specific desire.

Females usually respond best to feelings, but not always. Men often respond well to visuals, and some people are affected by audio. To learn which is the best stimulation to focus your persuasion, look at how they talk. Do they say "I see," "I hear what you're saying," or "I feel that..."? These are prominent examples, and of course, the correct answer could be more subtle and perhaps a mixture of two types of stimulation.

Adjust your persuasion techniques based on the kind of mind you are dealing with; for example, when persuading someone who is "feel" orientated, focus on how they will feel if they do what you are trying to convince them to. Don't try and tell them what it will be like - you have to make them actually feel it.

The more you're aware of the person you're dealing with, the more effectively you will be able to focus your persuasive techniques.

Mirror-Based Persuasive Techniques

Matching your body language and even your pose/position is a subtle but surprisingly powerful persuasive technique. You need to be subtle, and it may feel awkward at first, but with some practice, you will see how effective this technique, known as "mirroring," can be at developing a rapport and easing persuasion. As well as focusing the content of your persuasion in a way that interacts well with their specific personality type, you can also adjust your language and the way you speak to put yourself on their level. People respond better to persuasive techniques that are in their own "language." Pick up on specific words that they use and use them back on them, especially adjectives. Pay attention to their speed, pitch, and volume, and respond as similarly as possible.

Other Persuasive Techniques

There are many other persuasive techniques that you can work on and build up. We recommend that you master the empathy/mirror persuasive techniques, most importantly, as these are the most effective. However, the following techniques can be valuable additions to your persuasion armory.

PERSUASIVE WORDS

There are many subconscious persuasive words that one can use. Often these will be a call to action: for example, "Do that" or "Be this." Positive words and adjectives such as "Definitely," "Most," and "Effective" are very persuasive all on their own.

Use "now" words such as "today" or "at the moment" often to subliminally suggest urgency.

RHETORICAL QUESTIONS

Getting the person to think for themselves is highly motivating and can, therefore, be extremely persuasive. Ask questions that engage them, and they automatically become more receptive. This will also help you learn more about them. Often this will even convince them that they are making the decision when in fact you have simply steered them to this persuasion.

EYE CONTACT

It is highly essential to develop a good rapport with the person you are trying to persuade. Without eye contact, this is virtually impossible. With consistent and non-threatening eye contact, you can develop trust. Add a genuine smile and persuasion will be much easier.

BE PERSUASIVE BY CONNECTING EMOTIONALLY, NOT RATIONALLY

Anyone in politics will tell you - people simply don't respond rationally. They respond based on emotions. To persuade someone, you must connect with them emotionally.

Aristotle identified the three basic elements of every persuasive argument:

- Ethos: the credibility, knowledge, expertise, stature, and authority of the person trying to persuade.

- Logos: the appeal of logic, reason, cognitive thinking, data, and facts.

- Pathos: the appeal to the emotions; the non-cognitive, non-thinking motivations that affect decisions and actions.

All layers are, of course, necessary, but it is perhaps the emotional layer that holds the most power of persuasion. We are emotional beings and are much more likely to be persuaded by the promise of feeling good than the promise of "something being correct."

Are Persuasion Techniques Moral?

Of course, you may be thinking that using persuasion techniques is immoral, underhand. Indeed, you may find yourself with the dilemma of whether to use them on someone you love. It's really up to you how you feel about using persuasive techniques but remember the following.

People should be aware of the techniques and know when others are trying to manipulate them. If you successfully persuade someone, you have simply out-competed them.

Persuasion is always optional. After much practice, you may find that these persuasive techniques simply embed into the nature of your being. Would you feel guilty for using any other aspects of your personality, such as speaking confidently?

Much of the time, you will be trying to do what is best for them anyway. The purpose of connecting with someone emotionally is to learn what they want. When you know this, you are only persuading them to do something that they will want to do anyway. So, by its definition, persuasion is not manipulation - it is just bringing your point across.

How to Manipulate People and Influence Decisions

Manipulation is not ethical, but in this dog eat dog world, we have to know how to manipulate people subtly and influence their decisions. Now, I'm not saying you go out there and manipulate everyone you meet on the street. Use these techniques for your own good. Sometimes you can also use these techniques to achieve positive outcomes.

With that said, we will see how to subtly influence using manipulation. While it is not possible to present a step-by-step procedure as every situation is unique, there are some guidelines you can follow to implement these ideas. Specifically, there are three things you need to be aware of to get what you want successfully.

First of all, you should try to inject a strong emotion when trying to manipulate someone. It could be greed, fear, desire, or any such emotion. If you don't do this, then people will start to think clearly, and your chances of success will be remote.

Another thing you need to know is the hot buttons of the person you are trying to manipulate. By carefully observing the person, you will know what his/her hot button is. It could be a pet, hobby, or a strong feeling about a subject.

Finally, you need to be aware of social engineering techniques. Hackers use this a lot to gain access to highly secure systems. For instance, if a person in a police uniform asks you to move away from a place will you go and examine if he is really a cop? We are conditioned to respond in a certain way to certain people. Like this, there are several other social factors that you can use for your own benefit.

Body Language And Its Impact

Human being's personality is projecting his or her image depending upon their posture. It is the body language that reflects the, which finally leads to its outcome. The result is directly proportional to the thinking pattern of an individual. Consequently, it could be a positive or negative performance. It is a major concern to an individual who is affected by social behavior. Therefore, the need is to evaluate physiological factors, which will affect the harmonic changes.

The posture is essential as it conveys a lot of information to others about the personality and behavior of a human being. The posture which is the body language communicating to others their behavior pattern. Consequently, it transforms into the stature, which could be high or low.

The harmonic changes taking place in human beings determine the high or low performance of a person. These factors are 'testosterone' and 'Cortisol.' The important aspect of these changes distinctly establishes the role of a person. This, in turn, will eventually change the body language.

Analyze and Persuade People

Analyzing the above factors; it establishes how it affects men and women in their performances. Chronically, women feel fewer performers than men. The physiological and biological factors make women weak as compared to men; however, exceptions are the rules. On the contrary, men who are, at the outset, are strong yet their negative thinking and fear factors make them non-performer and vulnerable. This substantiates the argument in its totality that nonverbal communications can decisively cause a change. The physical or body posture can change the entire scenario favorably or otherwise as deem fit.

Amy Cuddy, a social psychologist, says that non-verbal conversations change the way we think and feel about it. She, further, says, "Our bodies change our mind; however, it is also a fact that our mind changes our body too." Evaluating the arguments reveal that a person's harmonic change takes place, thereby changing his behavior. It can increase testosterone or cortisol level, making them high or low performer respectively. The other aspect of non-conversational behavior is that a high-power person's testosterone level increases and decreases the cortisol level. It means the powerful people achieve a high position at the same time control the stress level.

On the other hand, people with a high cortisone level go in the depression, thus becoming susceptible in their outcome. It is important to control the cortisol level to become effective and successful. Can this be achieved in a short span? The answer is 'Yes'; it can be done in a matter of a few seconds. When your stature reflects a high performer posture, it then signals to others that you are an achiever.

Understanding The Psychology Of Body Language

Body language has been known to have a significant impact on interpersonal relationships. Even simple hand gestures can be interpreted in several different ways. To complicate matters more, other body movements and facial expressions can change the meaning of a hand gesture. Therefore, it may not be as easy as it seems to read body language.

People often do not realise it, but their body movements are an example of erratic behaviours that can give away their thoughts to others. Because different personality types exhibit different behaviours, you need to be conscious of how you move, as many times people can measure you by the behaviours you display.

Analyze and Persuade People

It's important to remember that the gestures we call body language not only tell us a lot about other people, but these physical expressions of what we are thinking can tell us more about ourselves as well. Body language might be described as a mirror to the soul because what we are feeling is reflected in our posture and physical movements. How we carry ourselves can tell others what emotions we are experiencing.

The exciting thing about non-verbal communication is that it is a product of our biology, environment, and culture. Maybe that's why body language can cue others about our attitudes.

We may inherit certain traits, which influence how we project ourselves to others, yet we tend to use different forms of non-verbal communication depending on our relationships with others. For instance, you likely present yourself differently to colleagues at work than you do to your family members. Perhaps because the comfort zone varies, you become more cautious in particular situations, affecting how you react.

No doubt there is power in the way that you physically present yourself to others. While some gestures are intended, many of the body's responses when we communicate with others seem to be more involuntary. Unfortunately, unconscious body language sometimes causes us to reveal things that we do not want others to know about us. Some physical signs can give others clues about our emotional state or about what we might be feeling.

Whether we realise it or not, we observe and process the body language of others, especially when talking. Facial expressions and hand gestures add more meaning to the conversation. If we were not aware of these things, another person's words probably would not have the same impact.

One way to interpret the signals of others more accurately is to become more conscious of your own. Pay attention to your gestures and movements as you talk. Try to see the connection between your non-verbal communication and the words that you use to express a thought. By learning to read your body language, you can begin to have a better understanding of the interactions, which you have with others.

Children are a prime example of how our natural body language works. Young children especially frequently communicate their feelings in a non-verbal way, even after they begin to develop vocabulary. You can usually tell by a child's actions if she is upset or unhappy.

Toddlers and preschoolers seem to have a natural aptitude for expressing themselves physically. Likewise, babies and young children become very good at reading our body language.

Interestingly enough, the gestures that children develop as a way to communicate their needs may help their brains develop contributing to verbal communication later on. From the start, infants pay close attention to an adult's face focusing on the eyes when you talk to them. How do they know to do this? Genetics is the most logical reason, so perhaps the eyes are the windows to the soul!

Read People's Minds
❖ **I See What You're Saying**

The premise here is that when we communicate, the words we use in conversation amount to about 40% of all the information that is being conveyed. The rest is all non-verbal communication. By using our awareness and developing our abilities of perceptual acuity, we can train ourselves to perceive and register minute details of other people that we interact with. We can learn how to see the facial tics, hear the pauses, watch the eye movement, pupil dilation, changes of skin color, nods, shrugs, micro-expressions that last for tenths of a second, among many other "tells" that most people are largely unaware of doing, and we almost never see. What looks like ESP or mind-reading is doing "a read" on someone's non-verbal communication. The trick is in knowing how to elicit and observe these signals so that they are meaningful to us.

❖ **The Set Up of the Exercise**

To create an exercise for expanding one's perceptual acuity, use a regular deck of playing cards. By using cards in an experimental and playful setting, we can create an impersonal context or environment where micro-expressions may be elicited, observed and used in "guessing" a target card.

The task of the "mind reader" is to try to observe any cues that give away the identity of the card as they mention the various attributes of the deck.

The task of the subject is not to mask, thwart or otherwise deliberately misdirect the attempts of the reader to pick out certain micro-expressions of the face and body.

They should strive to be sincere, and open. The objective of the subject is to mentally project a clear thought, in this case, the card that they selected. There is no competition or testing. It's merely a skill-developing exercise, comparable to practising scales on a piano.

❖ Pick A Card. No, Not That One!

Spread a deck of cards so that you cannot see the face of the cards. Have your subject select a card. Be sure that they get a good look at it. Direct your question to say the card, silently to himself. Encourage him to shout it quietly to himself. Tell him to picture the card.

They should keep their eyes open, but they can still see the card in their mind's eye. Have him expand it to the size of a poster, or a painting in a museum, or even to the size of a billboard.

Get him to blow it up big, really BIG. Silently bellow out that card, turn it into a cheer! Shout it, quietly in his mind and make the colours and the details of the card brighter, more vivid. The idea here is to get an amplified experience of that card.

As they hold that impression of the card, begin to talk about the choices you could make about the attributes of the card that was selected. Speak aloud as to whether it's a red card or a black card. Be sure they hear what you're saying and look for any betraying signal, twitch or sign when you say those identifying attributes.

When you say, for instance, "It could be red or perhaps it is black", they may look down, or their pupils might dilate when you say the attribute that matches the card.

Or they might pause their breath or eye blink rate for a beat longer. Keep repeating variations of that choice until you think you see an unconscious signal. Then when you make your decision of which colour it is, ask him directly if your choice is correct. Was it a red card? Then proceed with other paired and opposing card attributes.

A number card or a face card? Odd or even, male or female? Clubs or spades if it's black, hearts or diamonds if it's red, high numbered or low numbered. Don't just say "red or black ".

Work it into a sentence, make it part of a conversation and be sure to look for those signals each time you mention both attributes and pick the one that seems to get an unconscious response.

Analyze and Persuade People

Declare your choice and get a confirmation before moving on to the next set of options.

If you're unsure which of the paired different attributes is getting a response, keep working it until you get something.

Keep narrowing down the remaining card attributes until the only remaining possibility is the target card. The signals vary widely from person to person but once established for a given person, and the signs tend to be consistent.

Don't tell them yet what their giveaway is if you want to continue this exercise with this person. Once you tell them, it will be irresistible for them to edit their responses, even if they do it unconsciously.

The Benefits and Consequences of Efficient Body Language

What more can you accomplish with efficient body language?

Have you ever wondered what kind of information is available from your body, how important it is and who can read it? Did you know there is now a growing interest in profiting from learning to interpret this overlooked area of human behavior? What are the benefits and consequences of this trend?

Efficient body language compliments efficient organizations

One of the major focal points of the Information Age has been on streamlining operations and making organizations efficient. With the ubiquitous use of spreadsheets and management software, hardly any business process has not been scrutinized and re-engineered. Although much time, energy and frustration have been saved incorporating machines and computers into our lives and work, this intense focus on technological solutions may have made us blind to the information our bodies incorporate and express. Our body language can and often does contradict and even sabotage what our well-rehearsed mouths are communicating. Yet how aware are you of it when it occurs?

The power and promise of gravity

For instance, observe how efficient is the average person's relationship with gravity. Most of us take this incredible attracting force for granted. Indeed, who has time to care about gravity when there are bills to pay, products to sell, and people to meet? Yet, think about how powerful the pull of gravity is when it comes to holding our world together. It even holds our moon in place. You are then welcome to marvel at the incredible amount of energy many of us use to resist this unavoidable force. For just a moment think about how much better we could feel and how much more energy we would have, how much better we could express ourselves just by being conscious of and working a little more in line with the Force of Gravity?

Most of us pay little or no conscious attention to the level of efficiency we use aligning our posture with gravity's pull. Since curiosity is an unavoidable part of human nature, it was only a matter of time before focus returned to profiting from more efficient use of the body's language. What if that time is nowhere?

Reading Body Language Basics

Take a walk in a crowded place and observe your fellow humans and how they use their posture to:

- Walk or stand while leaning forward, backward or to one side and work against gravity.

- Hang their heads forward or backward conspicuously out of line with their center of gravity,

- Rock or waddle from side to side while walking forward.

- Aim their feet in another direction than the one they are walking towards.

- Wave their arms around much more than just to maintain their balance

- Shuffle so much when they walk that their shoes begin wearing unevenly?

Each one of these nonessential movements requires energy and effort to counteract the force that gravity imposes upon them purposefully. Also notice that small children use gravity most efficiently, yet as we age and become smarter, we tend to ignore gravity's pull more and more. Using one's own energy to resist gravity is totally unnecessary and insane if we are really trying to use our energy efficiently. If we are that blind to what our bodies are doing when it comes to our posture what kind of effect, conscious or unconscious, can this behavior have on those with whom we are communicating?

The Light's on, and Nobody's home.

Pay attention to how most of us seem oblivious to what our bodies are doing while we go about our day. Many of these movements are the product of being unconscious of our body language or being conditioned by society to ignore it. Regardless of the benefit or consequence, do something often enough, and you will create a behavior pattern. Once a pattern is in place, it doesn't take long to become part of your identity. For most of us, this pattern becomes incorporated into who they think they are. Even with an injury, if the initial pain you wanted to avoid disappears, the pattern and muscle tension is often forgotten and remains. Many go further by wasting even more energy and time by complaining about how tired they feel. Does this sound like an efficient use of our resources?

Efficient Body Language is often unwelcome information.

You are now invited to try informing someone of your observations. If you actually dare to take on this challenge, marvel at the responses you get. Most will politely excuse it away, often blaming an old injury. Others will become insulted that you would bring this up as this is "just the way they are." Note closely how many warmly thank you for your advice and begin immediately adjusting these inefficiencies. If knowledge is power, do you also sense an opportunity to learn something most others ignore?

Reflecting over Conscious and Efficient Body Language

Most importantly, you are invited to reflect over what people's' body language, behavior patterns, and their responses to your comments tell you about the individuals involved.

- Do these patterns make them appear more or less attractive?

- Would you be more or less inclined to hire them?

- Are you more or less interested in their advice?

- Does their age and intelligence seem to affect how they respond to you?

- Would you wish someone in your family to show these patterns or date someone who does?

As a bonus, ask yourself what does their response tell you about their ability to be curious, adaptive, and responsive?

What about your own Body Language Signals?

So far, we have talked about all of those other people surrounding you. Here is your invitation to stand in front of a mirror, take a reflective inventory on all the questions above, and see how they relate to you and your body language. What does your body language say? How quick are you to acknowledge and adjust it? By the way, how many of those around you may also know how to read it?

The Profit in understanding conscious body language

There is a gold mine here waiting for those who understand how to read, feel, and interpret what the body language of another is demonstrating. There is also a jackpot waiting for those who are aware of what their own body language is saying. There is a third jackpot waiting for those who understand that by adjusting theirs, they will not only feel healthier and happier, they will become more attractive and influential. Could your body language have something to do with your success?

How to Read Body Language - Top 10 Tips

Interested in learning how to read body language? Would you like to be able to tell when people are lying and understand people's intentions? This section will provide you with the top 10 tips for reading body language.

Body Language is the most important language you can learn. It bypasses the verbal communication barriers and gives you an insight into what others might be thinking, or what actions they are likely to take.

Remember that the art of being able to read body language is to be able to look at someone, pick up the signals, and at the same time not let on to that person you are doing this. If you do, the person will become uncomfortable.

Tip 1. - Eyes

Dilated pupils - the person is interested in the topic.

People say that the eyes are the windows to the soul. They can tell so much information about the person if you know what you are looking for. As in most situations, the same signal can be interpreted in a different way. It depends entirely on the circumstances at hand. The example above could also mean that the person is on drugs, or it could mean that they are focused on.

Tip 2. - Hands

Open palm.- the person is relaxed and comfortable.

The hands have many expressions and are a good place to start when learning how to read body language. Generally, when someone's hands are open, it means that their defenses are relaxed.

Tip 3 - Mimicking

When you are talking to someone, if they are mimicking your body position and action, it means that they are comfortable in the situation and most likely interested by you and what you are saying.

Tip 4 - Eyes

If someone's eyes are gazing to the side, it is a trait that they are feeling guilty. Likewise, if they are gazing down this express's shame, remember the eyes have so many meanings, and it's easy to make the wrong evaluation. Practice makes perfect.

Tip 5 - Arms

The main two expressions with arms are that they are either closed (folded) or open. When folded, the person is possibly angry or disapproving. When their arms are open, the person is in an honest position and is accepting of the situation.

Tip 6 - Rubbing of the Chin

If someone is rubbing their chin, it generally means that they are thinking.

Tip 7 - Feet

When you are in conversation with someone, you can tell if they are comfortable and interested in what you are saying by their feet position. When standing opposite one another, the other persons' feet are facing in your direction. This means that they are comfortable, and their head and eyes will also be focused on you.

When standing opposite someone, their feet are pointing away, and their head and eyes are not focused on you. They will most likely be nodding and agreeing with a fake smile. This means that the person n question is not interested and might even feel uncomfortable in the situation.

Tip 8 - Legs

When stood up, Legs are a good indicator of how confident someone is. If someone is standing with their legs shoulder width apart, they are relaxed. If they are standing with a stance wider than that, they are confident and are in a grounded position to show they are in control.

When stood up with legs crossed the person is probably shy.

When sitting down if the legs are crossed, it shows the person is in protective mode. This is very much used alongside crossed arm action.

If the legs are open when the person is seated, then they are in a relaxed position — the same as when standing.

Tip 9 - Fingers

Fingers can create many gestures and are great for reading body language. A pointing finger can either be someone pointing to an item or place, and it can also indicate anger. If someone is curling their fingers tightly, they are usually pleading for something.

Drumming or tapping with the fingers indicates frustration. The faster the beating, the greater the frustration and tension inside the person.

Tip 10 - Eyebrows

The eyebrows have many uses. Listed below are some examples. When the eyebrows are raised, normally the person is shocked or surprised. The greater the surprise, the more raised they will be. When someone flicks their eyebrow up and down quickly, they are greeting someone else or are showing they have acknowledged them.

The Art of Analyzing Faces

Face reading, just like body language reading, is an art. You need to be aware of the most common body languages for you to be able to decipher what someone really means when you feel like the spoken words are misleading. This is also true for face reading. Knowing the different features of the face, the shape of the lips, the size, and position of the eyes, among others, will tell greatly about a person's personality.

Although you cannot base all perceptions on facial features alone, learning to do face reading can prove beneficial in some aspects as well.

The face tells so much about a person's characteristics. If you have a thin and long face, it may connote that you are a very patient person and works hard to complete your tasks well. Generally, you are well-liked for your attractive personality. Round-shaped faces mean you are basically a happy person, the life of the party. If you have a broad face, it means you are passionate about the things you believe in and in general, are a very broadminded person. People with square-shaped faces are often times thought of as being aggressive when it comes to running after their goals.

If you have a strong jawline, usually, that suggests a determined personality. Having fuller cheeks indicate that the person is dynamic when it comes to his or her approach in life, while a jutted chin signifies the person is a bit obsessed about the self.

As has always been said, the eyes are the windows to one's self - and thus, says a lot about the personality of the person. Ironically, people with large eyes are often seen as warm, gentle, and more loving as a person. Small eyes signify that the person is detail-oriented and has clear-cut notions about things. If you know anyone whose eyes are very close with each other, that would mean he or she has a great sense of concentration and is a very energetic individual, while eyes that are positioned wide apart means a broadminded personality.

The lips also say much about a person's characteristics and traits. In general, people who have thin lips are described as workaholics and responsible, while fuller lips are for those people who enjoy life, know how to have fun, and are very much unperturbed in their lives. Smallmouths reflect a person's level of concentration. Thus, this would equate to an intensely focused person. Wide mouths, on the other hand, usually signify how much a person enjoys having new experiences in life.

The nose does not only "smell" someone's personality but also tells about a person's character. Small nozzles are usually associated with weak-minded people, and a curved nose implies the person is a bit self-centered and falters when he or she has to make decisions, and a large nose connotes a tough personality.

These are just some of the qualities that you can glean from people's facial features. They may apply to some people you know, but are non-conclusive of anything, because in the end, what you need is a special interface with another for you to be able to really "read" a person's characteristics.

It's in the Face

Most often, people think they can conceal their emotions flawlessly. However, with the exception of a certain few, many of our emotions are betrayed by our most easily identifiable feature: our face. Our expressions in particular usually give emotions away, and certain emotions have their signature looks on our faces, that are formed by some 60 operational facial muscles. They have been studied by a variety of scientists, in particular by Paul Ekman of the University of California Medical School in San Francisco. And due to the research of Dr. Ekman and people like him, it has been determined that only about one in ten people can convincingly mask their feelings as reflected by their facial expressions.

His work suggests that humans have some universal expressions or gestures that defy most bounds of culture. A smile, for example, would symbolize happiness almost anywhere you go. Having the right expression can mean the difference between looking confident, calm and accommodating as opposed to inaccessible, negative and snobbish, so watch out for those signals your body gives out that may not be reflected in your words.

When you find yourself in a spooky situation, and you feel afraid, for example, your eyelids partly open with the white of the eye exposed above the iris and the lower lid tensing. The eyebrows come closer together and raise, which gives wrinkles to the forehead. Your lips are usually tense and are pulled back.

And when you're happy, the tell-tale signs are dimples that run from your nostrils to the corners of your mouth, raised cheeks and wrinkles that are present underneath the lower eyelid or the corners of the eyes. Watching your emotions and keeping control over them through understanding is important because more often than not, these emotions will register on your face and can affect how people perceive you and how they deal with you.

How to Analyze Handwriting

Most people have heard of handwriting analysis, also known as graphology. It is a branch of psychology which relates handwriting to personality, emotions, and desires. By looking at a sample of a person's handwriting, a trained graphologist will be able to tell if the person is lying, feeling nervous, has low self-esteem, is depressed, is a narcissist, is generous and kind, has an artistic or analytical mind, is highly intelligent, is an introvert or an extrovert, has high libido etc... Handwriting analysis is widely used in forensics to profile suspects and in psychotherapy to delve into a person's subconscious. What most people do not know is that handwriting analysis is not as complicated as you may think, and with the right information, anyone can master this art. The following are some tips on how to analyze handwriting:

How to know if the person is stressed: Look at the upper loops of the letters b, d, f, h, l and t (these loops are known as upper zone loops). Normally, the loops will be slightly rounded. If these loops are angular or pointed in shape, then the writer has a predisposition towards stress, tension, anxiety, and frustration.

How to spot liars: look at the stems of letters. When writing normally, some retracing of stems will occur; however, if retracing is very frequent, then it indicates that the person is trying to conceal something. This is because the writer knows that he/she is lying, and as a result, their writing will be more intense. This tension will manifest itself in the handwriting, and it is generally believed that if over 35% of a person's upper zone strokes are retraced, most likely they are not telling the truth.

How to spot someone with fragile emotions: look for broken loops. Broken loops occur when the hand leaves the paper and is found in both upper zone loops (e.g., l, h, and b) and lower zone loops (e.g., p, g, and y). Writing with many broken loops indicates that the writer has a fragile or broken emotional state of mind. Marilyn Monroe's later handwriting is said to have contained many broken loops.

© Jacob K. Darren

[72]

How to Analyze a Liar by Observing Their Body Language Signals and Gestures

It is very important to have control over body language in order to lie successfully. Using the telephone, email, or by letter are the easiest ways for a person to lie and get away with it. The mind may be capable of creating a believable and convincing story to support a lie, but the body will have great difficulties in going along with it.

The body language will betray the mind in many ways because the subconscious mind always acts independently and automatically during a spoken lie. This is the reason why many amateur liars are easily caught before they can even finish their story. No matter how convincing they may sound, people will still be able to notice those giveaway body language signals contradicting against their words.

We have broken down these signals into categories ranging from those transmitted by facial expressions which can be manipulated by the mind if it is practiced, to the hardest to control and therefore the most truthful nervous system.

Face The Facts

Facial expression is considered as the easiest to control because we are always aware of what our faces are doing — therefore making the face the hardest part of the body to tell if a person is lying or not. But recent research has discovered that even with the high awareness of our facial movements, we have yet to master the visual expressions that can reflect our inner thoughts.

Before even the brain can send any message to the face of what it wants to say, the eyes are already sending out these little giveaways signals. These giveaways expressions are considered as reliable indicators that what is being said is in conflict with the true underlying feeling.

When looking someone straight in the eyes, most people will find it very difficult to tell a lie. They will look down, look away, or even glance at you very quickly. These gestures are most commonly associated with the term shifty-eyes that usually suggests confusion, dishonesty, and deception.

You must also consider that shifty-eyes does not always mean someone is telling a lie. He or she may be worrying, under pressure, or just confused about his or her own opinions or feelings. But what you can be sure of is that this person is currently unable or unwilling to disclose his or her true feelings and thoughts, and is trying hard to conceal this fact from you.

Lying Through The Teeth

Since creation, the telephone, unfortunately, has been a worthy instrument used by many people to lie. But luckily, you are still able to spot a liar using your ears alone. If you observe closely and carefully how the words are being spoken by ignoring the content, you may still be able to distinguish the truth from a lie.

Recent research has shown that when a person is lying, the voice actually becomes less resonant. When we are holding back from truthfully expressing ourselves, the normal voice will flatten, losses it's depth and becomes more monotonous.

Another fact is that people actually talk less when they are lying, and tend to create more mistakes in their speech. Unless they are those well-trained smooth-talkers (e.g., salesman, lawyers, politicians), they are also more likely to slur, stutter or hesitate as they speak.

Somewhere Over The Mouth

Children often cover their whole mouth when they are lying as if to conceal the source of dishonesty. This original childhood gesture is also one of the most used common adult gestures when lying.

When a person is lying, the brain will subconsciously command it to repress the untruthful words that are being said. The hand will be used to cover the mouth while the thumb is being pressed against the cheek. Occasionally, some people's gesture will only be several fingers over the mouth or even a closed fist, but its message remains very much the same.

On the contrary, should you see someone doing this while you are talking, he or she may be having difficulty in believing you.

Touching Pinocchio's Nose

When a person is not telling the truth, he or she will rub, stroke, and scratch the nose more often than one who is being honest and straight forward. One explanation is simply that the nose is just right above the mouth, and when the negative thoughts of deception enter the mind, the subconscious hand gesture to cover the mouth deflected to the nose.

Another ingenious reason is that lying increases tension and tension causes an actual physical itch in the nose. Hence, the scratching of the nose may, in fact, be used just to satisfy the itching feeling. However, there is a noticeable difference here as the genuine itch in a person's nose is normally satisfied by a more obvious rubbing motion, as opposed to a light touch or stroke of the self-doubt nose touching gesture.

Just the very same as the hand over the mouth gesture, it can be used both by the speaker to conceal his or her own deception and by the listener who is suspicious of what is being said by the speaker.

See No Deceit, Hear No Doubt

Rubbing or touching the eye area is a very strong indication of doubt and deceit. This gesture is the subconscious way of the person's mind trying to avoid looking directly into the eyes or the face of the person to whom he or she is lying.

When telling a lie, a woman will usually rub just below the eye gently in a small and light gesture. This is either because she wants to avoid smearing her make-up, or it might just be a typical woman's gentle gesture as to how they were brought up in a feminine environment.

Compared to a woman, a man usually rubs his eyes in a more robust gesture. However, if the deception is a huge one, men and women will both share a similar gesture of avoiding the listener's gaze by looking away at the floor or the ceiling.

Coming over to the hear no doubt side, rubbing, twiddling or tugging the earlobe is a sign on uncertainty or confusion which, if performed while a person is talking, signals a lack of faith and trust in what is being said by the speaker. And again, It also means that the listener isn't convinced of the truth of what is being said by you if performed by another party while you are talking.

These ear touching gestures are actually the improvised grown-up version that originated from the both-hands-over-ears gesture used by young children who wants to block out his or her parents' naggings and scoldings.

Truthful Feet and Legs

During a conversation, when someone chooses to lie about something, he or she will most often cross arms or legs concurrently. It indicates advance self-defense against any future challenge.

Other common foot signals may include constant foot tapping and feet pointing to the exit. These gestures are suggesting that the person is having a desire to escape the current situation and wants to get out. When a person is trying to get out of something, it normally leads to fabricating a small harmless lie instead of having to tell the truth in situations like not wanting to come to work or attend a particular social function.

The Honest Posture

The body posture of a person who's lying is often stiff and controlled. The person's natural physical expression is being held back when he or she is holding back the truth.

Research confirms that people are less likely to touch or sit very close to you when they are being dishonest. There is also a high possibility they will turn their whole body away from you to hide both their face and the truth.

The further postural language which clashes with the spoken word may be seen socially when someone pretends to agree with you, and the fact is that this person is just unconvinced underneath and is rejecting both you and what you are saying.

The Stressful Signals

The stress signals of the autonomic nervous system are the most reliable pointers or indicators of dishonesty and insincerity. Stress reactions such as sweating, face paling, and uneven breathing patterns are quite impossible to conceal or even to fake it.

The most common and reliable indicator of lying is the dry mouth, and this stress reaction will cause the liar to lick his or her lips more often, and also swallowing nervously at certain times. Occasionally, there will also be more throat-clearing than usual.

These stress reactions are caused by the heightened sense of fear of someone when he or she is lying. Such obvious stress symptoms normally only occur in the event of dramatic circumstances.

Piecing It All Together

Judging from the body gestures that have been described here, concealment is probably the better word than lying to define the main influence behind all of them.

It will take a considerable amount of time and observation to acquire the ability to accurately interpret and differentiate the many types of gestures in a given situation.

Every nose-rubbing or ear-tugging does not necessarily mean that someone is outright lying deliberately. These so-called gestures of deceit can also be initiated from someone who is just simply expressing doubt, uncertainty, confusion, exaggeration, or apprehension.

Having the ability to pick the correct underlying mood of a person's gestures is the real skill of interpretation. This can be achieved by analyzing the other types of signals right before the display of those mentioned gestures and interpreting them in context.

It is also very important to consider what culture someone comes from, the personality type, and the actual situation the person is in. Some cultures may not be uniquely expressive, while others may be dramatically demonstrative. Always remember to consider the whole picture and not just that one or two isolated signals.

Analyzing People By Eye Movements

Your eyes will position themselves according to the thoughts that are in your head. By watching your eyes, other people can often tell what you are thinking and if you are lying.

Professional poker players know that your eyes can be a dead giveaway. Most professional players are very good at reading body language and are keen on reading them. They also tend to wear sunglasses, ball-caps and other accessories on their faces to hide their eyes.

The behaviour of the eyes is relatively predictable, someone will make eye contact with you, and during the conversation, they take a moment to think. For this brief moment while they access information in their brain, and their eyes will move to a predictable position. Here are what the different positions mean:

❖ **Eyes in the Upper Right (1st person upper-left)**

When someone walks their eyes up, and right it means that they are accessing the visual part of their memory. In this person's head, they are visualising objects, colours, movements, and other visual information that pertains to your conversation. If you want to see, someone does this a good question to ask them is, "what colour is your car?"

❖ **Eyes to the Middle Right (1st person left)**

Moving the eyes directly to the right is a sign that they are accessing the auditory part of their memory.

The person could be remembering a song, the sound of a voice, or a particular noise. If you ask someone to think about the sound of their alarm clock they should look to the right.

❖ **Eyes Down and Right (1st person down-left)**

Someone that is talking to themselves or thinking about what they are about to say next will look down and to the right. Ask someone how a conversation went and they will look down and to the right.

❖ **Eyes Up and Left (1st person up-right)**

Looking up and to the left allows someone to access the visual part of their imagination. This person is constructing a picture in their head. If you ask someone to imagine a green sky with red clouds they should look up and to the left.

❖ **Eyes to the Middle Left (1st person right)**

A person seeking directly to the left is constructing sounds in their head. They may be imagining what a quiet voice sounds like or putting together a new melody. Ask someone to image the sound of a car horn underwater, and they will likely look to the left.

❖ **Eyes Down and Left (1st person down-right)**

When thinking about their feelings, someone will look down and left. Often when people say "I feel..." They will glance down and left, and you can know they are thinking about how they feel.

To detect someone that is lying it is essential to understand how their eyes usually move and then take notice when the behaviour of these changes.

For instance, your friend is telling you about his recent vacation and is looking up-right while describing the hotel and the places he visited.

Suddenly his eyes move to the upper left, and he tells you about this girl that he met while he was there. There is an excellent chance that he is lying about the girl.

Many people have become good at lying by learning to mask the signals of a lie. If you watch their eyes, they will likely maintain eye contact while telling a lie or will shift them away from you. Once again, notice how they were moving them when they were telling the truth and then compare this to when you think they are lying.

How To Easily Read People

The best part of the process and steps that you are about to read is that it is a lot easier to do than you probably realise. If you can begin to focus on these steps, you will be able to read people's nonverbal communication better.

❖ **Step 1**

Look deeper. When you meet someone, make sure to look deeper than what is being presented. You do this by reading body language, and subtle cues. When you look deeper, you aren't judging the person, but instead, you are getting a feeling of what the person wants to go.

❖ **Step 2**

Read subtle cues. Subtle cues are the cues that you get when the person is not looking in your direction. Is the person moving a lot, or are they still? Do they seem to look nervous? The first impression you get is the best, follow that impression and work from there. Look at the nonverbal cues that the person continues to present. Read into the situation with your intuition and gut feelings.

❖ **Step 3**

Be present. A lot of times when you are focused on the present moment, you will be allowed to read the cues better. When you are not focused on other things, body language is more accessible read.

Take a look at the person's posture and see if they want to close or open up. These are all good cues to reading body language. The more present you can become the better your chances of feeling out the other person.

Reading People's Thoughts
❖ **To Read the Thoughts**

The idea of reading the thoughts of other people has been one of those things that have been a topic of discussion for many years. Indeed reading other people's thoughts is one of those things that everyone has encountered many times during life.

Many times you may have been thinking about a close friend or a loved one, and the next thing is that they call you on the phone or visit you.

It could be easy to call things like this coincidence but if we consider that there may be more to this universe than meets the eye. So what is the truth about reading other people's thoughts? And is it possible to read the thoughts of another person?

❖ **The Power of Communication**

It has been said that when you speak, the words only communicate a small percentage of the information. Some of the more critical aspects are the tone of the voice and body language. Indeed the tone of a person's voice and body language can show when someone is lying.

Have you noticed when a person is lying they find it hard to make eye contact, so this points to the fact that spoken communication is not the only way that we communicate? Have you looked at the idea that birds fly in perfect formation even though we do not perceive them communicating? So do we have the ability to communicate on a psychic level? And could it be the case that we all can relate on a psychic level?

What Can We Learn From The Near Death Experience?

There was a story of a man who had a near-death experience when he was 16 years of age but had an interesting story about his experience. Following the event, he appeared to become more psychic, so when people asked him how he became psychic, he gave this answer. He said that you do not become psychic, you are psychic, and you choose to forget you are psychic to make this earth experience more realistic.

So could this suggest that we may have the ability to communicate using thought communication, and is this a skill that we can develop? And perhaps we may even be able to create this by using methods like meditation. So does a psychic ability have links to the ability to read the thoughts of other people?

❖ **Good Relationships**

It has been found that when people are in close harmony, they tend to pick up the thoughts that each other is thinking, this tends to suggest the importance of having a good and close positive relationship. In NLP the suggestion is that by exercises such as matching breathing two people can build rapport.

So the idea of reading the mind of another person could be initiated by some form of mental permission giving. If this is the case, then the idea of reading the thoughts of another person may be associated with the building of trusted relationships. So have you experienced thinking about a close friend and then being contacted by them, and have you found that a close friend has been thinking the same thought that you have been thinking. Ideas To Make You Think.

The Power Of Persuasion

Reading people means that by just looking at that person, you already know what kind of person he is. Through this, you already know how to approach that person. For example, a guy is courting a lovely lady, before that guy starts to the court that lady, he will first observe her and study her by just looking at her. Asking some questions from her friends also helps a lot, but it takes time. That guy wants to get her on that same day.

❖ **The first tip is observed and plan**

Analyze and Persuade People

It is the first step in gathering the information and to formulate your persuasion strategies before you attack.

The information you are gathering here is the character and attitude of that lady. An example is, look at her actions, her friends, is she talkative, how she dresses, and just like that. Another example is when a lady likes a guy, what do you usually see from her? Ladies will start to get the attention of that guy, give a beautiful and sweet smile or even seduce that guy. Are that true ladies?

❖ **The second tip is read the facial expression and emotion**

This time, you already made some actions, strong actions to get what you want. That lady made some effective efforts to draw the attention, ignite the emotion of that guy an easily gets what she wants.

These strong actions may include conversation if you apply this to marketing and sales.

And the third tip is harvest all you want. After reading people instantly, it is not already challenging to get what you want. The question is, can you master and learn reading people immediately in a concise time?

© Jacob K. Darren   [91]

Tips For Reading People And Interpreting Gestures

Reading people and their body language can give you great insights into their real feeling. We use our head, arms, hands, shoulders and even legs and feet to make gestures, and emphasise what we are saying, but the majority of gestures are made with the hands and arms. Here are some things to look for, to help you interpret body language and gestures.

1. Nodding or tilting the head to the side shows interest, active listening, and concern.

2. A head held up indicates confidence, but if it is held too high, it can indicate aloofness or a patronising attitude looking down your nose at someone.

3. Shrugging the shoulders with a palms-up gesture indicates that the person doesn't know or care, or is bored or uninterested.

4. People sometimes reveal their real feelings through body language that contradicts their words.

For example, if someone says he agrees with you, but his head moves slightly from side to side, he is signalling disagreement. He may be showing his real feelings, but not want to be bothered arguing with you.

5. Some people pick lint from their clothing. Whether this is conscious or unconscious, it can indicate that they disagree with you, but can't be bothered to argue.

6. Nervousness often shows in your hands. People who are anxious may rub or wring their hands together, or clasp and unclasp them.

7. When we aren't comfortable with our hands, we hide them in our pockets or behind our backs. Hands in the pocket convey a hidden agenda or secretiveness.

8. An open palm suggests honesty and sincerity. A closed fist can be considered menacing.

9. Hands on the hips can be seen as defiant.

10. The fig leaf position, with your hands, clasped together over your crotch, or folded tightly over your chest (the female fig leaf) can make you seem aloof or defensive.

How to Spot Romantic Attraction

and Respond Appropriately

Signs of romantic attraction are among the most important questions of men and women today. In this busy world where crossed signals are still common, some people mistake gestures and body language as signs of romantic attraction, only to fall flat on the face when rejected.

There is a way to tell if there is a romantic attraction between you, and you don't even need to blatantly ask if there is.

Romantic attraction is usually felt by the parties involved. But if both are too shy to finally break the ice and at least make a connection, the signals are usually lost into oblivion.

On the other hand, the signs of romantic attraction could also be squandered when one party overanalyzes the innocent gestures of another and makes moves based on this assumption. Thus, it cannot be emphasized enough that you should know the signs of romantic attraction.

Analyze and Persuade People

A good way to tell that another person is attracted to you is an increased interest in you. Does he or she want to know more about your life? Then chances are, the person likes you. But while this could start on a friendly, less intense level, this could soon turn into something truly romantic when encouraged.

After the liking and the interest, the person may seem to want to spend more time with you. And to sweeten the deal, you like spending time with this person too! When there is an intense enjoyment of each other's company, you can be sure that the signs of romantic attraction are already budding.

When you want to take the relationship to a deeper level, make sure that the signs of romantic attraction would not blind you to the flaws of the other. While flaws are ever-present, make sure that these flaws are issues that you can see yourself living with and helping the other overcome.

If the person is set in his or her ways and would never be open to change for the benefit of the relationship, then you may have to reconsider taking the relationship further. While feelings are very real and valid, a relationship is more pragmatic than just the giddy butterflies-in-the-stomach feeling.

Bear in mind that while you like the person very much, you have to think in terms of ten years down the line. If you see yourself possibly hating the person by then, then leave the friendship as it is.

Always remember that to enjoy life fully, you must surround yourself with genuine, positive people and positive relationships. Though the tough times may come, you know that these people would be with you through to the end.

As in the case of friendships, so should your romance be a haven of positivity. Enjoy the signs of romantic attraction as it comes, but always temper it with a wise and pragmatic assessment of the other's positive and negative traits.

How To Read The Body Language Of Your Date (Signs She Is Romantically Interested)

It is a fact that women send out an estimated five times more body language signals than men. However, men do not understand them as quickly as women understand body language. Women are expert in sending signals which may be sexual or emotional; used for attracting a person or informing him that they dislike him.

A man has to be quick to understand the body language of a woman he is out on a date with. Look out for these signs:

A distinct smile:

A girl's smile can be of many types; from a flashy smile to a ravishing one. While in conversation, if you happen to look up and catch her eye, and she smiles and looks away. She may be embarrassed. If she smiles continuously chances are she is not being too polite.

Hair play

A woman playing with her hair also called as preening, is a sure shot clue that she is interested in you. Twirling it, flipping it or tucking it behind the ears is a good sign. These signs are the most common signals of flirting. Look out for these on your first date.

Body language

If your date crosses her legs, uncrosses them and then directly crosses them in the other direction, be aware that she is flirting with you. If her leg is crossed towards you or her shoulders are angled towards you then consider these as good indicators of expressing her interest in you.

Sensuous Lips:

Most men find a woman's lips quite stimulating. A woman may send signals by eating slowly as it brings attention to her lips. Wetting her lips quite frequently indicates that she may allow you to pay closer attention towards her lips, that is she will allow you to kiss her sooner than later!

Frequent glances

It has been rightly said that the eyes are windows to a girl's heart. If the glances are too frequent, or she is looking at you the way she has never looked before, chances are very high that she is interested in you.

How To Read The Body Language Of Your Date (Signs He Is Romantically Interested)

You are acquainted with a guy and have been on talking terms with him, yet you do not know if he is romantically interested in you or is he just being nice and decent. To know if he is romantically interested you will have to do some face, mind, and body language reading. Here are some signs that will tell you his true feelings.

Greets you warmly

Whenever you meet him, you get the feeling that he is genuinely pleased to meet you. His greeting is genuine, and there is no hint of formality in it. When he sees you, he comes towards you with a smile that reaches his ears. Lack or absence of phony greetings means that is romantically interested in you.

Never leaves an opportunity to prove how good he is

If he is constantly trying to impress you with either his good behavior or with his special talents, then it means that he wants to be romantically linked with you. He will not do this with other girls.

You figure in his discussion all the time

Because he is romantically interested in you, he can't get you out of his mind. He will be discussing you with his friends and colleagues. Even his family will know a lot about in spite of never meeting you.

Wants to meet you often

He is so smitten by you that he will attempt to meet you on the silliest of pretexts. This he will do at the cost of him appearing desperate and childish. Well, he does not want to lose you and hence wants to be near you all the time so that he can ward off any competition.

His touch says it all

When he does shake your hands or holds them, you will notice that he does so for longer than usual. He will do this subconsciously as he likes you and due to his romantic interest in you. He will also try and make physical contact whenever he can.

Takes you away from the group

If the two of you are from the same group, he will attempt to take you aside and do stuff with you. He will also ask you out for coffee without making it clear that it is a date. He will want you to be with him only, and he will try to wean you away from your group.

Thoughtful gifts

Unlike your other friends, you will notice that his gifts are thoughtful and romantic. You will receive special attention when he is celebrating special occasions and when it is your birthday, or on New Year's Eve, he will be the first one to wish on the stroke of midnight.

How To Read People Like A Book

One of the most significant mysteries of humanity is discovering the secret to how to read people's minds. If you could read people's thoughts, you could know precisely what another person is thinking. The power of mind reading tricks and techniques lies in your ability in how you are reading the behaviour and signals that the other person gives you.

Here are the secret ways to read people's thoughts through body language. When you know what a person is thinking, you are in possession of authoritative knowledge that can help you lead interaction in your favour.

Reading body language is easy and fun. Most of us don't do this consciously, so we fail to recognise just what a great mind reading technique it is. Here are some things to watch out for to get you started:

If they are facing you, they are listening and paying attention to you. But if they are turned away, they are not focused on you. If they are rocking side to side, they are impatient and want to end the conversation. A curved back is a sign of deliberately ignoring or avoiding someone.

Analyze and Persuade People

When someone backs up, on a subconscious level they feel threatened and are retreating from you. If someone is gradually moving towards you, they are interested in you or what you are saying.

Pointing their knees or their feet towards you is a universal sign they agree with you, they are aligning their posture to yours.

If they begin to mimic your body language, that is a sign that you are leading the conversation.

Crossed arms are a sign of defensiveness or contempt, the exception is when the thumbs are visible and pointing upwards, that means they are feeling detached but amicable.

If their hands are facing you with open palms, then they are open/receptive to what you are saying.

If eyes look upward to the left they are trying to create an image out of nothing. They are actively using their imagination, and this can be a sign that they are making up whatever they are telling you. If their eyes look upwards to the right, they are trying to remember a particular image, access a specific memory. These are just the usual guidelines, some people, primarily the left-handed, have the opposite eye movements, so it's essential to get a baseline reading by compelling them to remember something that you know happened.

Most of these things we will feel during our interactions. Without paying conscious attention, we will start to feel when a person is becoming defensive and only then notice their closed body language. Learning to pay attention to your feelings is an easy way to start growing more aware of what the body language of others is telling you.

Aside from sociopaths and habitual liars, deception is stressful. When we are stressed out blood circulation is prioritised to the essential organs and diverted away from the extremities. If someone is lying, they are very likely to have cold hands. This stress will also make the person more jumpy in response to a loud noise or some other startle. But just remember, fear does not imply deception.

Eye contact when we are lying is not natural, but it can be forced. If a person starts making strange eye contact that feels off, then they are probably angling something shady.

The way a person is thinking will be reflected in the words they use and the questions they ask.

Analyze and Persuade People

Someone who likes to talk about social situations and relationships is someone who is very focused on interpersonal relationships and will respond much better to interactions that incorporate those elements. Relationships are based on emotions, and these people will be swayed more by emotional arguments than logical ones.

By paying attention to all the signs a person is unknowingly giving off, you will seem to be reading their mind. These techniques will give you an awareness of what others are thinking that you may even start to surprise yourself with your accuracy.

Most people are so focused on what they are about to say next or what they want out of interaction that they are only diverting a minimal amount of their attention to the other person. When we focus our full attention on what the other person is doing and saying, we gain tremendous insight into not only what they are thinking, but how they think.

❖ **Listen for the tone, volume and the words that are being used**

A loud voice and threatening words are warnings that the other person wants something to be done. They may be demanding and talk using strong terms. They may interrupt, and you will need to be careful so that you speak at the most appropriate time. On the other hand, some people are hesitant about stating what they need, and you may have to coax them into telling you what they are thinking or feeling. The tone of voice, volume and words are all good indicators of the person's mood.

❖ **Consider patterns**

If you have known someone for a while, you might recognise specific models that they use. For example, they may be individuals who wait until their time with you is ending to tell you exactly what is on their mind.

Some people who seem to be unreasonable when you first meet with them will calm down after a rant if they think that you have listened to them and wanted to help them. Past patterns are an excellent way to predict what the person might do or say next.

❖ **Ask right questions and focus on the response**

When you deal with a situation in a direct manner and then carefully assess the replies you will likely be able to develop an understanding of the person's perspective. Be careful though in your assessment. One-word answers might be either hesitancy or disguised anger.

Understand People Better

Body language is non-verbal communication but is used along with verbal communication. It expresses our emotions, conveys our attitudes, demonstrates our personality traits and supports out verbal communications. Everyone uses this whenever we communicate with each other.

Many non-verbal behaviours vary across cultures, such as the thumbs up to signify "way to go" or "good job". However, the six primary emotions, happiness, surprise, sadness, fear, anger, and disgust are shared amongst all cultures. These six are instinctual and are not body language we are taught, but come from within us naturally. When we talk about body expression coming from within us we mean, it comes from the subconscious level. And because it comes from the subconscious, it tells a great deal about the person we. Let's look to fear for an example.

Fear

Fear is a natural human emotion and serves a purpose related to our safety and security. But let us imagine a person who has witnessed a severe automobile accident, but rather than running to the aid of the injured; they run frantically in the opposite direction.

This frantic running away is body expression that indeed infers some fear. Specifically, what that fears might be we cannot know without talking to the person.

But it is evident that the fear has nothing to do with immediate safety. Through this example, you should be able to see how we can read another's personality through the lens of his body language.

Here's an experiment you can try at home to see just how much information people give about themselves through body communication. While someone is talking to you observe the body language they use as they speak. After a few moments of observation, close your eyes while continually listening to the other person.

You won't be able to see their hand gestures, facial expressions, or other bodily movements. Notice how much information is not available to you because your eyes are closed. It is challenging to read and understand someone without seeing the body expression that accompanies their verbal communication.

Analyze and Persuade People

One sure-fire way to learn how to read someone's body talk is to observe and get to know your own. Remember, we all have six common kinds of instinctual body language.

Of course, they vary in degree of expression, but we all have them. There are also non-verbal communications that are common to particular cultures, societies and families. Because of this fact, two different people can have very similar behaviours that are expressed through same kinds of body communication. By knowing your body language, you can read similar ones in others, and therefore give you insight into another person's personality and who they are.

As you learn your body language, try to relate those behaviours to your subconscious thinking. Try to regulate or over analyse your unconscious thought though.

The only goal here is to match those thoughts with the body language you use to express those thoughts. This not about judging yourself, but it's about learning to read your body language so you can understand the body language of others. You can use this information to improve your understanding of the many different interactions you will become involved with.

© Jacob K. Darren

Now that you recognise some of your body languages you can begin to read people with more accuracy. When in conversation with someone you can identify such things like mixed messages. Mixed messages are defined when a person says one thing, but their body communication means something else.

A good example is when someone lies to you. They tell you, "I didn't do it!", but the tone of voice, the looking away, and the slight nervousness lets you know that something is not quite right in what they are telling you.

This conflict between verbal language and body language could signal deception. Mixed messages are most certainly related to insincerity and point to that person as having something to hide.

Analyze and Persuade People

Things You Can Do To Analyze

People Better

1. Practice moving your focus of attention during conversations so that you become almost a detached observer or video camera watching you and the other person talking. It means shifting the focus from you and what you're concerned with to the bigger picture of what's happening in the space between you.

2. Take notice of how they engage in conversation and whether they tend to initiate things or wait for others to start. You are looking for clues as to where their focus and energy is so noticed if they tend to think before speaking (an inward focus) or bounce ideas off others (an external centre).

3. Consider how they describe things and how much detail they give. Do they tend to use short phrases just to give a flavour or do they give lengthy descriptions with lots of specifics about situations? It tells you how they work with data and how they like to gather information.

4. Mentally record whether they tend to talk about things in a logical, objective way or use words and

examples of feelings, values and motives. Listen particularly when they are describing a decision or choice they have made and notice whether there were personal issues considered or just logic and rationality.

5. Notice how they seem to think about time and planning. Do they seem to have a structured way of working and organising themselves or do they seem to enjoy a more spontaneous and flexible approach? There are clues in their descriptions and thoughts about plans, projects and work deadlines.

6. Use your information from the previous four areas to form pictures with keywords that describe the person you are studying or reading. Outgoing or Self-Contained? Detail Focus or Summaries? Feelings or Logic? Organized or Spontaneous? The will help you engage with them in a way that they are comfortable with.

7. Notice when you are talking versus listening and get used to doing much more of the latter. Don't jump in with a "that reminds me of" personal experience of your own. Become focused and curious about people and build mental pictures as they speak then ask questions about the pictures.

8. Ask questions which are about more than facts and basic data. Develop some words which you are comfortable with which ask people about what their thinking is concerning something they've just said or how they feel about a particular topic they have raised. Keep building your pictures from their answers.

9. When you have built a basic relationship with them, (you'll know because they answer your questions about their thinking and feelings) consider asking a "Why" question. These are more personal so don't be in a hurry. Your purpose here is to start understanding their values and what's important to them.

10. Keep checking your initial judgments and observations with your mental video camera switched on and noticed whether there is evidence for what you guessed or assumed from the earlier conversations. Test your assumptions by asking questions or just listening to them talk to others and noticing how they are speaking.

Basics Of Reading People

Words are universally used in every language to express and communicate with another person; they are known to be the means to describe one's feelings, thoughts or expressions. But sometimes, people communicate in an unspoken language which is known as body language.

Where words fail, body language helps describe a person's feelings, expressions, thoughts and reveal part of their personality. If a child is in pain or he/she is sulking, they will cry, throw tantrums, stomp their feet to show they are not happy about something. Same way adults have various gestures to show what they are feeling without uttering a word.

Here are some classic examples where body language reveals a big part of person's personality.

People are suffering from insecurity and complex touch themselves in some way consciously or unconsciously as a mean of self-defence and self-comfort. Crossing arms, rubbing forehead, hugging self can be few such gestures to reveal such personality as these gestures provide them protection.

People in despair & depression reveal their thoughts by drooping their heads or eyes, by slouching in their steps, their body sagging while walking. Opposite to it, a happy person or a confident person will walk tall, there will be a bounce in his steps, and the posture will be upright to show his positive attitude. The body naturally shows such signs, and it's not a conscious effort to reveal what mood a person is in.

Sometimes it can mean someone is just thinking or reflecting sitting with a drooping posture. If someone is thinking hard or absorbing information his head with most likely rest in his hands or fingers.

A rigid expression can mean the person is holding back something he wants to say but cannot say aloud or trying to reveal it through physical gestures. It can also mean the person doesn't want to talk and expressing it without saying much. Sometimes people are standing in the way that they don't want you to move in or out and have no intention of moving. Few such gestures are folded arms, crossed legs or pressed lips.

If you find a person stiff means, there is something he wants to say but holding back and revealing it through their bodily gestures. The signs may be subtle, but they show enough to know a person or a personality.

How To Read A Person's Personality

It is difficult to understand what a person is and what kind of personality does that person posses. Why we need to read people is because usually, people trust such persons who are not supposed to be believed.

And when they trust such person, there are significant losses that are suffered at the end. But you can't do anything since it's too late to apprehend him/her as that person may have escaped and can be difficult to find in that case.

There are many cases like there are people who trust someone as for as the business is concerned. Since they have blind trust by the past performance but that is not enough. The person's personality is like a whole book that can tell you all that you want to know.

To know all that you need to develop the following skills are have to follow the following way or procedures to identify what kind of person is he/she that you are trusting or talking to or in other words what kind of personality does the person have. The following is what you as an ordinary person, a skilful or intelligent person is supposed to do:

❖ Observe by forgetting what has he done in the past
❖ See how he walks
❖ Observe every moment of that person
❖ Find when he/she is angry
❖ See the behaviour when alone
❖ Observe the difference when the candidate talks to you and with others
❖ Notice the things that he likes in your absence
❖ What kind of environment does he live in?
❖ What does he wear?
❖ Way of spending
❖ Language and accent in speaking
❖ The company he or she is living in
❖ And then:
❖ Notice the structure of the hands
❖ Notice the facial expressions
❖ Observe and notice the movement of the eyes

If you see nearly all these things, there will be an answer that will automatically upload in your mind, and you will finally declare it yourself whether the individual is a Mr. nice or not. It works everywhere, like in relationships, at work or in business.

As the facts and figures that you have gone through runs in your mind, you will understand that who and what is he/she and above all what can be predicted out of this candidate or what kind of things this person can do in future that is good or bad. It is how you can effectively and efficiently read anyone.

By seeing in a person's eyes for long with concentration and depth, you can quickly read the person's mind, and that will lead you to read the person, personality.

Analyzing People Through Their

Stories

If you were asked about communication that caught your attention, was easy to remember and inspired you to action, what would come to mind? It's unlikely that you thought of a spreadsheet or even a PowerPoint presentation. It is likely that whatever you remembered had a strong story component.

Analyze and Persuade People

Stories are the way that human beings take the building blocks of fact and create a structure that has both meaning and momentum. We tell stories as naturally as we speak and we listen to them with heightened perception. We are good at evaluating the truth inside the story.

Start small. What do you talk about when you're making small talk? Fans tell stories. You might be a fan of a sports team, a hobby or a reality TV show. Any of these interests will inspire you to tell stories about who is doing what to whom and what results different people are getting and who is winning or losing.

You might be telling stories about what people want or about who people want to fight. You might be saying stories that consistently end triumphantly or badly. As you hear the consistency along with the stories, you can begin to wonder what patterns of cause-and-effect you are learning as you talk and listen.

It's not so much that the stories you tell say a lot about you (although they do). It's more than the stories you tell are the stories that you are giving your attention: when you say stories about your team, your neighbour, or your favourite show, you are repeating a pattern until you learn it.

© Jacob K. Darren   [120]

Analyze and Persuade People

You can learn that third time's the charm, that the right die young, or that power always corrupts: you can learn it from telling stories from different parts of your life about different people who all share a standard message or pattern.

Whatever you are saying about the things that interest you, you are probably also saying about your work life. Whether you believe people are buddies who get you through the tough times or adversaries who are bound to slow you down, you believe it in all your stories. If your stories are about turning adversity into victories, then you will see the next cancelled project or economic downturn quite differently than if your stories are about how small problems snowball into bigger ones.

Since most motivation is unconscious, we are better at justifying our actions than we are at predicting them. Listening to our stories gives us better clues about what it is we are likely to choose, and how we are likely to respond to stress or conflict. If you tell stories where people get beat up and then bounce back, you will find that you have more resilience when you are facing difficult times. It is true whether you spontaneously tell stories, or you just give them your attention when you encounter them in media or other people.

Unbelievable Way Of Reading People

Of course, listening to other people's stories gives you the same kind of window into their motivation. Have you encountered people in your work life who consistently turn small problems into bigger ones, people who seem doomed to repeat their mistakes? They probably tell a lot of stories characterised by a dramatic imbalance of power.

Although the main characters in their stories struggle bravely, they are doomed unless they can fly under the radar of the powers that be. It does not mean the tellers will stay under the radar: it does mean that they will expect to be doomed whenever they become conspicuous.

There's a song that asks "how can a loser ever win?" A loser who tells stories about losers is unlikely to change his luck. A loser who tells stories about winners is just at the bottom of an upswing, ready to make decisions that get better results. When you listen to the stories around you, you get better at predicting who will persist through difficulty, who will stir up conflict, and who will stick with a challenge long enough to break through to something better. Predicting these and other behaviours requires more than analysis of the facts: the same events make some people and break others.

Stories are the difference that makes the difference. Listening for patterns in the stories people tell is one way to reconcile their behaviours and the way they justify those behaviours.

Through stories, you can see some of the patterns that work through unconscious processes to determine how people behave and motivate themselves. You'll gain a chance to read people better, to put them into situations where their stories are an advantage, and to change your own stories to improve your odds of success.

Easy Persuasion Steps

If your goal is to hone and perfect your persuasion skills, you can approach it just like other projects. Most projects require several steps during a certain time frame to complete. A project as complicated as training your mind to become more persuasive naturally requires preparation, know-how, and perseverance. It will take several steps over a period of time. Setting out to persuade people is not an exception. Choosing to get what you want is not any different. Here's how you can persuade people and get what you want in 5 easy steps.

Step 1.

Establish Strong Credibility. This will be important because one of the primary things that you should create in order to make a believer out of every doubter is credibility. Cite a credible source that is known to be an expert in the field where you are trying to convince someone into believing. If you want to convince someone to believe in what you say cite a known and credible source and present your arrangement that agrees with that source.

Step 2.

Focus On Positives. This is a very critical step. It demands concentration as well as your full attention. It might be best for those who could do it this way: When learning how to convince folks you have to learn how to concentrate on the positives in an argument. People have an aversion to negatives, and in order for them to trust you, you have to focus on the helpful aspects of what you are trying to say. The reason that this is important is to present people with profit and advantages that are realistic because the more feasible your arguments are, the more people will have faith in what you have to say.

Step 3.

Offer Solid Proof. The skeptic's mantra is "to see is to believe," and this is what you have to focus on in order to win people over. Another significant strategy would be to find facts that will support your cause or back up your arguments. Presenting folks with proof will eliminate their doubts, and they will believe you more.

Step 4.

Be an Expert. To elaborate on that a bit, people will always trust experts and recognized people before they do you. To build credibility, you have to be in line with well-liked experts and use them and what they say to your gain.

Step 5.

Stick to the Facts. Just make sure that you always stick to the facts. Do not fabricate data or makeup things in order to win over people since that will not do you good in the long run. You might think that you can get away with it, but there is always the possibility of running into someone who knows better, and you risk exposing your lack of credibility.

Happily, after you have followed the above steps religiously, you'll have unlimited success and will then experience the fruits of that success! You should congratulate yourself and allow yourself to become satisfied and slightly proud. You set out to "Conquer this Monster," and today you have done it! Revel a little bit in your accomplishment.

Let's Consider Persuasion Hypnosis

When you think of hypnosis, you typically think of it as being extremely powerful and even a bit manipulative. Most people think of it as a way of controlling someone and getting them to do things they usually would not do. What you need to understand is that there are several different forms of hypnosis.

One of these forms is persuasion hypnosis, which really is nothing more than an indirect method of sub-communication. The whole premise behind using this type of hypnosis is to establish a rapport more effectively with other people.

Have you ever thought about what it might be like to hypnotize someone? Think about what you may be able to achieve if you could sell more, persuade others, and seduce the opposite sex just by using a few simple techniques.

The process of using a few simple words and commands during the regular conversation to persuade and influence others is known as "persuasion hypnosis" and is also known as "conversational hypnosis" or mind control. Once you become familiar with the methods of persuasive hypnosis, the techniques almost become second nature. You can easily incorporate the methods into your daily life to achieve higher success in both your professional and personal life.

Think about all the ways persuasive behaviors influence your life right now - sometimes without you even knowing it. For example, when you see someone yawn, it makes you yawn. When a person crosses their legs or scratches an itch, you will sometimes do the same. All of these things are similar to persuasion hypnosis. Your body is subconsciously mimicking the behavior of another.

This isn't just some hokey internet scam either. These practices are based on a real science known as neuro-linguistic programming or NLP. But how can learning these techniques affect your everyday life? Well, say you are a used car salesman, by using these powerful hypnotic methods, you can use simple language to convince your customers to buy from you. Or, perhaps you are not a lady's man but desperately want to find the woman of your dreams. The good news for you, in this case, is that the art of persuasion can be a powerful tool if used correctly.

There are many programs available on the internet that claim they can teach you the art of conversational hypnosis. The best advice is to be very careful with your hard earned dollar. Many of these are just courses are scams and do not follow through on any of the promises to teach you the correct methods. This is not the type of thing to be taken lightly. These tactics can be very dangerous when used by people with harmful intentions.

The Easy Art of Conversational Hypnosis

How to persuade people? It is much easier than you may think. Sure, there are some advanced techniques, but there are also far more many easy techniques too. This section of the book will share some of them with you and also explain why you must learn this to gain the upper hand in the game of life.

Somehow we wonder why some people have that great ability to persuade us to do something we initially won't do if we are left to decide for ourselves. Indeed, the power of persuasion is amazing, and we want to learn how to persuade people - because we find it helpful in our business, in getting more sales, in lobbying our cause, or in getting others to do what we want them to do.

Learning how to persuade people can be done through conversational hypnosis, sometimes called covert hypnosis. Unlike the usual hypnosis thing in which a person is assisted to go into the trance state, or you are aware that you are being put into hypnosis, conversational hypnosis is a hidden one. It may only involve casual conversation, and you may not detect that you are drawn into the hypnotic state. We may think that some people just have that charisma that they are able to persuade, but they can even be into conversational hypnosis even if they themselves do not know it.

Persuasion Everywhere

Let's first dispel the myth that covert persuasion is difficult to do. Look around, and you will see that it is all around us, and most of us don't even notice it every day.

Ever chosen a brand of beer over another because of a commercial? You may not think so, but the brewers spend millions of dollars every year, making sure that you do.

Ever met a person and felt an instant connection to them? It is not your intuition at work. Whether they intended it or not, their body language was probably responsible for it.

How Covert Hypnosis Can Benefit All Of Us

Why do we want to persuade people? Because every conversation we have with someone (except family and friends) is usually an attempt to gain agreement. Sometimes there is a battle, and you may win some, and you may lose some.

Imagine the greater success in life that you can have if you know how to gain the upper hand ever time - getting a better pay rise, bartering down a product, seducing someone you like, gaining agreement in meetings and much more.

Example Technique - Hand Gestures

Hand gestures are a great way to subliminally persuade people. Most people make hand gestures when they talk, but the listener rarely looks at their hands. This is an opportunity to embed commands and make implicit suggestions.

For example, at an interview, you may want to convince others that you are the person to hire. First, you need to discover the interviewers "no" direction. When people talk in the negative, they will point in one direction, left or right.

Then, as you talk about good people, including yourself, you should gesture towards yourself. As you talk about other people who are not as good as you or any negatives, you should mirror the gesture that the interviewer makes.

This is a highly effective technique that works really well.

Example Technique - I Have A Secret

This is a great example. Think back to when someone has told you a secret. They say, "look, I'm not supposed to tell you this, but." Think about what you thought of the person telling you this and the information. Most of the time, a secret becomes highly credible due to the way in which you hear it.

You can use this to persuade people to take a course of action. Salesmen do it all the time - they say something like: "look, I'm not supposed to do this, but I'll give you a great deal on this car, just don't tell my boss about it, OK?".

Immediately you establish rapport, and you think you are getting an absolute steal. In actual fact, the boss has probably told him to use this technique on every customer!

This technique can be powerful, but it can also be quite difficult to master. Most often, this type of hypnosis is used in sales and businesses where it can help you in managing your business as well as dealing with your customers. However, the unethical use of conversational hypnosis is discouraged. That is why effective and special training on this hypnosis technique is made available only to a few.

Conversational hypnosis is done by putting together powerful words, and phrases including tones, intonations, and gestures into messages that can influence the subconscious of the person being hypnotized. The basic steps followed in this type of hypnosis are establishing trust with the subject, misleading or confusing him and giving him suggestions while in the confused state.

Active listening also is an important skill in learning how to persuade people. For some, they use this skill in hypnosis by simply using your own words to persuade you. It may also involve the use of positive words as well as repetition, although techniques in using this method have also evolved over time.

Conversational hypnosis can be found anywhere today, mostly from businesses who want to get good sales - from TV ads and other forms of advertising that somehow have those hidden 'magnetic' power that persuades the people to buy. Some individuals who can carry a conversation well and public speakers who can amaze and solicit action from the people could also be having the skills of covert hypnosis. Those who are in counseling may have also used this technique in hypnosis. Skills in covert hypnotism may have been used as well in building great relationships and in managing arguments in the family or at work.

Covert Persuasion - Simple Secrets to Hypnotism

What exactly does covert persuasion and hypnotism have to do with each other? First of all, we should start with mainstream hypnosis. That is the most common form, and most of us have seen it before. This is where a volunteer or group of volunteers go on the stage and are hypnotized to think they are chickens. They cluck around on stage, and it can be very funny for everyone watching. It is what most people think of when it comes to hypnosis. There another form of hypnosis that is much more persuasive and has been outlawed from being used for advertising by businesses. This is called covert hypnosis, and you have probably never heard of this.

Before we can really understand the art of covert persuasion, you first need to understand the three basics of covert hypnosis strategy and the related science. There is hypnosis, neuro-linguistic programming or NLP and mentalism. Each of the three goes hand in hand to produce a discreet form of persuasion. Using these techniques together, they are extremely powerful and work without others knowing what is really going on. Just learning any one of these techniques is amazing, but learning all three can be life-changing.

Here are the basics of each of the three and the relationship to covert persuasion.

Hypnosis is simply the art of hypnotizing people. This method is where people are put in a trance-like state, then suggestions are planted in their minds. This is the method you have probably seen at live shows and on TV where people are made to act like chickens. This is also used as a supplement to help people give up smoking or shed extra pounds. This skill is effective and can be used to help people attain of conversation. It is basically establishing a deep connection with people, and getting them to want to work with you. This can be used to put people into a good mood and make them feel really euphoric and relaxed whenever they are near you. With this technique, the possibilities are endless on what you can obtain when people want to get things done for you. Spreading the work will be easier than ever, and people will be excited to help.

Mentalism is the third form, and it is the art of creating false realities. This, in effect, is causing people to believe literally anything you suggest to them. Some of the best illusionists and entertainers around the world use this, and you have possibly seen this on TV as well. It even goes as far as some of the faith healers out there using mentalism techniques to make people believe that they have been healed.

These three techniques combined you will be able to obtain dominance over everyone you meet. You will be able to make them do almost anything or believe almost anything you say and usually with only needing to say a few words. These same methods could be used in dealing with the opposite sex to create attraction almost instantaneously. You will become a skilled bargainer and always get the best deals possible. The most veteran sales person you buy from will be convinced they need to give you a discount. Customers will buy from you just to have the chance to be around you.

The most exciting aspect of using covert persuasion is that you will learn how to make people around you feel better about themselves. This knowledge will make people so excited to be around you; it will almost be like they are your loyal servants. You will be able to provide people a comfort they will not be able to find anywhere else, and the benefits will be in your best interest.

Covert Hypnosis - Persuasion Techniques

Covert hypnosis sounds like some kind of secret black ops technique, but it is used more in the corporate world than anywhere else. It is a way to influence others without them, realizing that you are controlling the conversation. So if you want to learn covert hypnosis then pay attention to this basic conversational hypnosis technique.

Introduce and listen

The first step is to introduce yourself and lead to the next step of them introducing themselves. Ask questions to let them talk as much about themselves as possible because the more that you learn about them, the easier it is to use that information to your advantage. Be sure to take note if they use visual or auditory language such as "I see what you are saying" opposed to "I hear what you are saying" because this makes a big difference which will be explained later on.

Build rapport and connection

Once you have been talking (more accurately listening) for a while it is time to build a connection with them, and this is as simple as agreeing with certain issues that they obviously have a passion for. So for example, if they talk about mortgage interest rates rising and you can tell this is a major issue then agree with them and reassuringly touch them in a non-offensive way like a tap on the shoulder. This confirms that you are listening and the physical touch helps you to convince the other person that you are listening and creating a trust, or connection, between each other.

Steer the conversation

Now you have the other person connecting with you it is time to start talking a little more. Remember the visual and auditory ways of talking? Now use the same method, which is a style of subliminal hypnosis, because your 'subject' will accept more information unconsciously this way. Steer the conversation towards your objective, and one of the best ways is to use the other person issues as the driving wheel. So let's say that you are trying to convince someone to invest, but they are worried about interest rates. The next step is to say "I see (hear) what you are saying about interest rises and you are right, in fact, now would be the perfect time to invest because of the way the market is moving." This covert method of persuasion is amazing because you are giving them the position of power; however, you have steered their decision process.

Mastering Subconscious Persuasion

To Attain Everything You Want

The subconscious persuasion is a matter of great importance because if you master it, it could help you out of numerous unfavorable situations. Well, different people use different methods of persuasion to get others to do the things they want done, from the use of excessive force, a cajoling tone, and perhaps by use of strong words. You could employ persuasion as an instrument at home, workplace, and so forth to achieve your different goals in life and more so, attain the happiness that you have always hungered after.

Having the power of subconscious persuasion will place you in a position to gain insight into when the tricks of persuasion are being used in you. What you should know about the power of persuasion is that mainly because you employ your internalized ability of persuasion and that of reading other people' minds and gestures. These things make the whole process such a breeze, with wonderful results guaranteed.

Mastering subconscious persuasion to attain everything you want

You probably have many tools that you can use in the mechanics of the initiation of the subconscious persuasion process. First, you should look at the voice you use. It has been proved that the use of a voice that is a tad lower when conversing with someone is more effective when you want to appeal to their subconscious mind. Using a low voice has the effect of relaxing that person, and more importantly, it would lower their defenses. Eventually, that results in establishing trust in these people.

Subliminal technology as a therapy

Subliminal technology is one of the most successful therapies that can be used to enhance the power of persuasion. This is because this one is aimed at the brain and better yet, it is always important to remember that every function that happens in and the body are controlled in the brain. Therefore, researching for more information is the key. There are many resources about subliminal technology. They will show you how it can be used to enhance subliminal persuasion. Know as much as you can.

Analyze and Persuade People

The following are essential techniques for mastering subconscious persuasion.

The framing technique

No better way to change your method of categorizing, sorting, associating, and eventually giving meaning to all aspects of life, from objects to events or even behaviors, than this one. Framing has the effect of swaying people towards your perspectives. To frame arguments that are persuasive, use words that will conjure images in the minds of those you are addressing.

The mirroring technique

This is mimicking the actions (the body language and movements) of the party you are engaging in persuasion. What you do is create a sympathy sense by playing the role of the person listening. This technique, also known as the "Chameleon Effect," is more effective because you employ it subconsciously.

The timing technique

Experts have proved the Subconscious Persuasion as being particularly effective when employed to people after a rather brain- cracking activity. Before putting a conversation with a person about something they are likely not to agree to, consider starting that talk when that particular person is mentally exhausted.

The reciprocation technique

We are greatly compelled by the good actions that are extended to us by close people in our lives. Probably, if you do something nice to your neighbor, at home or at the workplace, they will also do you good for reciprocation. What you will achieve by this is that you will complement these relationships by the power of the Subconscious Persuasion.

How to look confident and

dominant

Many people ask themselves how to look confident, yet they don't understand that self-confidence isn't about looking confident. Confidence is a state of mind.

However, there are three simple tricks that can make you appear as a confident person AND improve your self-confidence at the same time. And that's how you should work on your self-confidence - improve both your outer game and your inner game. Here are three things that you can do to improve your overall confidence.

Get off the couch and transform your body

Get off your couch and start working out! When you'll lose some body fat or gain some muscle, you'll definitely feel more confident. And not only that - you'll also look more confident! Have you ever seen a shy bodybuilder? Even if you don't want to look like a bodybuilder, transforming your body and making it look more healthy will definitely improve your self-confidence.

Analyze and Persuade People

Does your posture manifest confidence? If not, you have to change it. When walking, try to be as tall as possible. Align your neck, back, and heels. Keep your chest forward, don't round your shoulders (keep your shoulder blades back) and keep your head up high. Shy people usually look down when walking - don't do it unless you really have to.

To learn how to have a posture that manifests confidence, you can observe confident people. It's a good idea to watch some movies portraying James Bond. Each actor that portrays Bond is a good example to learn from.

Change your clothing style and take care of your body

No matter what people say, they DO judge you by your clothes. If you have never paid much attention to your clothing style, the chances are that you don't dress well. Maybe it's time to change or at least improve your clothing style? Go to a clothing store and try some new clothes!

You should not only pay attention to your clothing style, but also to your body. Take care of your skin (especially if you have acne), sleep more, start eating more healthy, exercise more, get a routine check-up - all of these things will help you improve your health. As a result, you'll feel (and look!) more confident.

Slow down and relax

If you live your life in a constant rush, you aren't able to savor it. Happy people know how to slow down and relax. You should also learn how to do it. Slowing down not only makes you enjoy life more, but it also makes you feel more confident - it's hard not to be nervous and insecure if you are in a constant rush. Slow down and rest a while and your self-confidence will definitely go up!

Remember that in order to look confident, you have to feel confident. All of the things listed above will help you improve your self-confidence and help you look more confident. However, it won't happen if you don't take action. Now it's time to change your mindset: instead of asking yourself how to look confident, ask yourself what you have to do to develop self-confidence!

Again, watch some James Bond movies and start observing his movements. He usually walks and speaks slowly and is almost never nervous. People who walk and speak slowly and do things deliberately give the impression that they are confident. Why is that so? Because most confident people are very deliberate and good-tempered. That's how to appear confident - slooooow dooooown.

Don't hesitate - use the "three-second rule."

Confident people don't hesitate often. Whenever you hesitate, you appear as a person who doesn't know what he wants. Learn to become a decisive person. Be proactive and determined. Force yourself to make fast decisions to strengthen your ability to be decisive.

You should also use the "three-second rule" that says that whenever you want to do something you're afraid of, you have to do it within three seconds. Do you want to approach that beautiful girl at the bar? Act in three seconds - just go and start a conversation with her. Do you want to ask a question in public? Don't hesitate - do it now! These small things will make you a more decisive, and as a result, more self-confident person.

The better you are, the more confident you feel - improve yourself

Make sure that every day, you are a better person than you were yesterday. When you start concentrating on improving yourself, you'll stop caring (that much) what other people think about

© Jacob K. Darren   [147]

you. Consequently, you'll feel more confident. And not only that - improving yourself will make you feel better about yourself (satisfaction from becoming a better person). Every day try to do something new, get rid of one bad habit, create a new one, or learn a new skill!

Smile and be positive

People who smile often are happier. Furthermore, they have more friends and have a richer social life in general. Consequently, it makes them feel more confident. It's hard to be shy if you have many friends, right?

Think about it: when you meet a new person, and he or she smiles a lot, you like this person more. He or she makes you feel good - and that's what confident people do.

If you want to appear confident, learn to be an optimist. Smile more often, be positive, make other people feel good. What goes around comes around - making other people feel better will make you feel better (and more confident) as well.

Improve your appearance

People who look good are usually more confident than people who don't care about how they look.

Don't get it wrong - looking good doesn't have anything to do with your genetics. Looking good simply means taking care of your body, clothes, health, etc.

One of the most important things that you can do to improve your appearance and self-confidence at the same time is to start lifting weights. Working out will change your physique and change your mindset - you'll feel stronger, physically, and mentally.

How to Appear Confident?

Is it something that can be learned? If you are asking yourself these questions, let's answer the second question first: yes, you can learn to appear confident. It's not that difficult, and you can definitely learn it in a few days if you take it seriously. The key is to make some simple changes in your life.

67571689R00083

Made in the USA
Columbia, SC
28 July 2019